BROADWAY JOSÉ

D1445934

Mitchell Belacone

The following is a fictitious account of a story based on some real events. The characters in this book are products of the author's imagination. Any similarity to real persons living or dead, including those living that you and the author might wish were dead, is coincidental and not intended by the author.

CONTENTS

Preface to the Preface   v
Preface: Apples to Empanadas   vii

Broadway José: Life as a Gladiator   1
Viva los Vikingos!   21
She Can Play Center for Me Anytime   31
A Shared Epiphany   40
Toros I: Taking the Toros by the Horns   45
Stallions I: Admittedly, I Wanted My Warm Blankie   49
My Home Away from Home   52
Everybody Comes with Disclaimers   54
Lobos I: Rabid D-Line   61
Aguilas I: Loyalty, Shmoyalty   64
Gladiators I: Bittersweet   69
Stallions II: "Oh, My Poor Leg Is Tired"   73
National Team vs. Paraguay   82
Aguilas II: Bombs Away   93
Gladiators II: Wannabe Spoilers   99
Lobos II: They Still Can Bite   102
Toros II: A Negotiated Outcome   104

The Play-offs: Vikingos vs. Aguilas   106

The Finals   114

I Got Nationalized!   122

About the Author   145

PREFACE TO THE PREFACE

The preface serves as a back-story to the football drama that unfolds in the narrative itself. "Apples to Empanadas" concerns itself with the rationale and motivations for transplanting myself into the Third World. The described differences in customs and culture between the United States of America and Argentina in the following preface should add clarity to the story.

PREFACE: APPLES TO EMPANADAS

I was born and raised on the Upper West Side of Manhattan in the 1960s. That circumstance use to make me think I was better than those who weren't. From my roof, where I played as a kid, I often looked toward the skyscrapers of midtown and thought how fortunate I was to be living in the center of the universe. On returning from summers at camp in Connecticut, when I got close to my apartment I would take a few strained breaths due to the amount of soot and the particular pollution of my neighborhood. That in turn would trigger a feeling of bliss knowing I was almost home. The city was my nicotine.

As coveted a place to live as many consider it, I was motivated to leave in 2003. Although it had become a safer and cleaner place than the Manhattan I grew up in, it had lost the major portion of what I and many natives considered its soul. The ethnic neighborhoods that I loved to explore as a kid had been almost entirely replaced by one big neighborhood comprised solely of people who could afford it. There are hordes of recent settlers in the mostly different-in-name-only parts of this borough that would tell you otherwise. To judge their opinions fairly, you must consider their limited experience and viewpoint. Eavesdrop on their conversations at restaurants and if it's not about what they are earning or paying for this and that, it's about what somebody else is. (Don't get me wrong, I'm no better. Me is enough of me; I don't need to be around people the likes of me all the time. I am not a self-loathing New Yorker; I'm a New-Yorker-loathing New Yorker.) The characters who I enjoyed listening to while growing up had been replaced with battalions of stroller pushers yapping between texts in coffee bars about the methods they were employing to make their children as competitive and neurotic as themselves. No easy task. I swore if I heard one more mother brag via a complaint about paying fifty K a year for kindergarten, I would never drink another coffee in public without noise-cancelling headphones.

Valerie, a friend's wife, happened to be in my neighborhood one warm and sunny Saturday with her two-year-old son Mark. We waited and finally got an outside table at . . . call it "Baby Carriage Central Café." Twenty minutes later, Valerie asked me to keep an eye on her kid as she went back inside to the line for a refill. About five seconds into my given task, Mark realized she was gone as I did my stupidity for not offering to go stand in the line for her. That type of screeching is bad enough coming from other people's tables; at mine it was painful.

I continued my foolishness in the form of baby talk, "Awww, c'mon, Mark. She'll be right back. Do you want my cookie?"

Upping the decibel ante: "Whaaa! Whaaa!"

I spotted a couple of noses looking down at me. As if their kids never wailed in public . . . As if I was a party to the birthing of this twenty-five pound noise machine. Oh, okay, keep staring . . .

Going by seemingly daily media reports at this time in New York's history, it appeared that baby-shaking was in vogue. I spoke loud enough so that every other table could hear me and warned, "Mark, I don't care if we are in a liberal neighborhood, if you don't shut it, I'm going to shake you!"

As a wave of dirty looks and disparaging chatter rolled my way, I surfed on top of it with a satisfying thrill. Only a twenty something black woman laughed. I don't know how funny she thought that odd crack was. I'm guessing she more enjoyed seeing a pack in the wolf's lair of American political correctness collectively punked.

Most cities I know have types of people I don't care for, but more and more I was finding New York's version the most unacceptable of all. I despise its culture of fear, with strangers rarely willing to engage each other in conversation. Granted, there are so many hostile and mentally ill people there that, if not a necessary behavior, it is at least an evolved one. Again, me is enough of the likes of me! Still the *What's the matter, you short on friends?* vibe that came my way in various innocent schmooze forays over the years pushed me in the direction of a map. In my last year there, I was trying to deny all of the above with this thought: *Maybe much of New York was really the same and it was I who had changed by suffering from the realism and cynicism that can come with age.*

At a bakery café I frequented, I ran into a childhood friend's parents whom I hadn't seen in thirty years. They were now in their mid seventies. John had been a journalist and Rebecca an artist. In the early 1960s, they bought a ten-room apartment on 86th Street and Central Park West when very few people wanted to. Accordingly, they paid very little. They made another wise purchase in a charming weekend cottage on Twin Lakes in Connecticut, also before it became pricey. I would guess, at the time, they did not see these so much as financial investments but rather quality-of-life expenditures made on behalf of their family. As we spoke of the people and interesting places we knew in common during our nostalgia fest, it brought me back to the New York I had loved and lost. To age eleven, when we visited friends of theirs in a huge un refurbished loft in SoHo, and how I had felt sorry for those people for their lack of walls and covered ceilings. I remembered seeing my first play at a children's theater in the far East Village when the neighborhood more resembled the Ball Prairie, exchanging tumbleweeds for strewn bricks and broken glass. We discussed our opinions of the changes that the city had seen. In spite of their unacknowledged status as real estate multimillionaires mainly because of those same changes, the only difference in our disapproving sentiments was that they were able to state more of them. I was too young to be outraged when the old Penn Station was torn down. It reassured me to have people I respected and admired parallel my thoughts, even if our chance meeting had turned into an impromptu wake for a city that—the reunion confirmed—was dead to me.

Where to move was the next step. I thought of Miami, Las Vegas, and San Francisco, but not for long. Too hot, too hot, and if I could not handle New Yorkers' rap anymore how could I deal with what passes for conversation in San Francisco? I was getting nowhere trying to think of a place in the United States that held more appeal for me than New York, which held little. I possibly could have found somewhere in the pastoral Berkshires to call home. For that to have worked, I needed a certain fantasy to play out: a woman who could be contented looking at me, books, and trees, and me looking at her, books, and trees all day every day, with maybe just a little Internet porn on the sly. Never found that. Mostly, I found women wanting to look deeper into me all the way to my tax statements.

"I need a classic six off Riverside Drive or Central Park West," a date once told me.

Then let a real estate agent buy you dinner, I thought to myself. *Now that you've priced me out, can I stop wasting your time and you my limited resources?*

The lady's comment in this interview disguised as a date was the final catalyst to my considering homes that needed a passport before a key to enter. Many people I had known had relocated to Europe including my boyhood friend from 86th Street. He worked and settled in Czechoslovakia when it was still commie. Back off,

Tail Gunner Joe! After sleeping in barns while selling tractors to farmers, he ended up being part of the Velvet Revolution. I wasn't looking for that much adventure; I was after bang for the buck and women who weren't—most of the time, anyways. Pardon the geographically specific misogynist tangent, but the type of girl who says no before she is even asked does not exist down there. The roundest of dudes can approach a ten, whatever the outcome; he will normally be made to feel better for having done so. A rejection, as most other social interactions, will almost by rule be handled diplomatically and politely.

Twenty-some-odd years earlier, I had considered Buenos Aires as a vacation destination for two reasons: It was called the Paris of South America, and it was dirt cheap. Between hearing that and making my way to a travel agent, it had become expensive again—as in *too* expensive. Forward to 2003: I read that Argentina had bellied up once again, re-rendering the place a bargain. A buddy of mine and I were soon on a plane to the Paris *sans* the nasty, to explore the possibilities. My friend, a world champion bargain hunter, landed in heaven. We were dining in top tier restaurants for around five dollars per meal. *Lomo* is the finest cut of beef. They butcher the cow differently, so there is no direct comparison. Back then, *lomo* for four in a high-end *parrilla* (steak house) cost nineteen dollars, the same as one Kobe beef hotdog I saw on the menu at an old-line New York Steakhouse before leaving. *Lomo* has almost no fat and tastes better than what passes for the best in New York. That con about marbling being good for flavor is only true for people who like the taste of fat and those who "don't know no better," as in Argentine beef. Argentina is the seventh largest land mass in the world with only around forty-three million inhabitants; they can afford to let the cows mow the lawn and not make a high-priced fuss about it.

Buenos Aires inhabitants are, on average, more cosmopolitan and wittier, and they handle stress better, than their New York counterparts. Here's why. Early last century when the Europeans migrated to Buenos Aires, they stayed put. The savior faire and humor that big-city living brings has been ingrained in them for generations. Their counterparts who landed in New York spread themselves to every state. Nowadays it's mostly the smartest and most ambitious of the following generations who return to conquer and proclaim themselves New Yorkers. A fair portion of those newcomers left *nice* back where they came from. They are often mistaken by visitors for the less common and more agreeable native New Yorkers.

Argentines are very polite and curious to learn about you.

"Where are you from?"

"New York, and I'm in the process of moving here."

"Is your job sending you here?"

"No, I just like it here."

Then would come three or four seconds of an incredulous stare, followed by a big smile, "Are you crazy?"

At that time, the Argentine *corralito* was in effect: Argentines were not allowed to withdraw more than the equivalent of a few hundred dollars per month from their own bank accounts while the government was devaluing their savings by roughly 70 percent. Translation: Their government stole 70 percent of their savings. What my inquisitive new Argentine friends failed to understand was that what made a living hell for them rendered me Mr. Big and all that I made go with that. What I failed to understand was a lot.

Buenos Aires is called the Paris of South America for its architecture, even if it's a hodgepodge of all varieties of European styles. I'm a fan. I was walking downtown and saw an old, ornate Italian-looking building that used to house opera people. It now served as a political club. I stuck my nose in and a woman approached.

In my butchered Spanish, I asked, "May I take a look around the lobby?"

In English, "Wait here for a minute."

She came back with a guy who offered to give me a tour. Fifteen minutes later, we got to the members-only restaurant. It was empty except for one table with seven or eight men drinking coffee. They were the board of directors. Various Argentine presidents had been brought to power through this club. They signaled me over and asked me where I was from. I told them and also let them know I was in the process of settling here. They invited me to sit down and have coffee with them. They asked all kinds of questions without being invasive, mainly curious as to why I chose Argentina. I had them chuckling, as I do most Argentines with my banter. If you are a native Spanish speaker and had heard my interpretation of that language, then you would know why. Those guys, like the majority of Argentine men, had the grace and charm of Italian movie stars. The president of the club handed me free tickets to a tango dinner they were having the next week. As a prospective resident, I was highly impressionable to all kindnesses and slights. I could hardly contain my delight with my new social standing. I tried to calculate how many lifetimes I would have had to live for something similar to happen in New York. It's not as if I could vote in their national elections; it was just their way of saying welcome.

I found a real estate agent to plan the next few days for me. She showed me a thirty-three hundred square-foot top-floor apartment in a period art deco building in Palermo. It was in one of the best sections of that neighborhood overlooking Palermo Park, with sole roof rights. On that roof was an in-ground pool. Don't think glorified spittoon, carved in there for marketing purposes. More like something you wouldn't be embarrassed to have in your backyard if you had a half-acre lot. The asking price was a negotiable three hundred thousand dollars. Real estate is generally priced in US dollars, because it would be unrealistic to price it in Argentine pesos. Even a short-term dollar value graph of the peso would resemble an electrocardiogram from a patient with a severe arrhythmia reading the bill of his last US hospital stay.

Next up was another top-floor apartment in the Palacio Estrugamou in a barrio called Retiro. I'm calling it The Dakota of Buenos Aires. It covered thirty-five hundred square feet, not including the chauffer's quarters and storage floor above. It was schlepped brick by brick from France, back when they could afford those extravagances. I wouldn't know if French turn-of-the-century bricks are any better than Argentine ones of that era, but it sure does make for good bragging.

The daughter of the lady whose apartment it was before she died (or who I feared was just lost and wandering around somewhere in it) noticed that I appeared like a serious buyer and commented, "My mother had an old butler who is an excellent cook, and it would make me and my two sisters feel better knowing he still has employment. He sleeps above in the chauffer's quarters, so you will still have three more servants' rooms."

Believing this none too subtle caveat could be a deal breaker: What was she paying him?

"Doing the conversion off the top of my head, I would say around $350 per month."

"Please inform him for me that he has a 20 percent raise starting the minute we shake hands." I chose not to add, *Also tell him, if his daughter looks anything like Audrey Hepburn, I can remake a low-budget Sabrina for him.*

On my way back to the hotel, I was trying to conceptualize myself in that place and keep my swelling head in the taxi at the same time. I relished the thought of inviting all my American friends, especially the ones I did not like so much. She was asking 325,000 US dollars. I took the agent's suggestion and offered 300,000. A Spaniard looked it at the next day, and it was adios to me and that palace; he took his own advice and paid the asking price.

Back in New York, I started to get cold feet. I had never heard of anybody moving to South America. The country had just pulled a Chapter 11, welching on the largest debt in the history of the world's nation's deadbeats. As late as the beginning of the 1980s, they were run by a military dictatorship. If I bought an apartment there, could Generalissimo Peron Jr. confiscate it?

In my lobby, I mentioned to a book publisher neighbor that I was looking to move to Buenos Aires. When we crossed paths a few days later, he asked, "Where are you moving to again? Guatemala?" I'm guessing he never had an interest in acquiring the North American rights to Borges.

When I relayed my plans to a young couple in advertising, the guy unloaded his fantasy of moving to a deserted island on me.

I'll be sure to pass on your dream to my eleven million new neighbors.

As an Upper Westsider, if I had told people there that I was moving to London or Paris it would have seemed no more radical than transplanting myself across the park to the Upper East Side. Argentina was incomprehensible, as it was on very few radar screens at that point.

I sold my eleven-hundred-square-foot pre-war New York apartment, put my furniture into storage, and moved into an Internet rental in Buenos Aires. The pictures online had looked much better than my new reality. I tried to analyze myself to ascertain if, by my doing all of this, I had lost my mind. My yellow Lab mix, Rosy, practiced her Spanish and *Evita* impressions off the balcony, and I continued my search for an apartment to purchase. An amigo of a new amigo led me to another apartment to rent while still on my search for one to buy. It was a seven-hundred-square-foot one bedroom in a newer building. Shortly after its construction, somewhere sat half of a mountain with its white innards and black veins exposed, having sacrificed its other half just to jazz up this lobby. It was situated in a high-end neighborhood, half a block from one of the nicest parks. Three buildings down was a palace-turned-museum with all the original furniture and artwork called Museo Nacional de Arte Decorativo. The guard house was converted into a café. Rosy and I often lunched in its garden. She had an inseparable soul mate for the past thirteen years in the form of a cat. He had died of cancer a month before we left New York. A certain day in the garden, Rosy spotted a stray cat. Her tugging enthusiasm convinced me to let go of her leash to see for herself if this was her missing best buddy. Each of three attempts to get close enough to play was met with a hiss and a swipe at her snout. She returned with a sad and confused look on her face, so I gave up a piece of my sandwich to distract her from the disappointment. As she digested her mozzarella and prosciutto, I did the fact that there was no yesterday or turning back.

My seventy-year-old landlord could not have been nicer; he invited me to a non-touristy tango with his buddies. The first time I needed a plumber for a leaky faucet, as a token of my appreciation and largeness, I did not pass on the bill; it came out to less than three dollars. He offered to sell me the place for thirty-four thousand dollars. I fumed to myself: *And where am I supposed to put the butler, in the boiler room? Sorry, no can do. Who is it the fuck do you think that you are to even imagine that I could live like that? The nerve!*

I ended up buying in a turn-of-the-century French building in a neighborhood called Recoleta. Roughly three thousand feet, over-twelve-foot-high ceilings, detailed to the point of making the Metropolitan Museum of Art jealous. Four bedrooms, four and a half baths, but with only two maid's rooms is what I settled on. It was even less expensive than the others. I paid in cash that was counted out at the closing table. That's how it's done. Bad checks and mortgage crises don't exist here because nobody takes checks and banks don't give mortgages. In a certain way, it's better. It keeps people from behaving like they have more than they really do and, thus, makes for less people owned by the company store.

After living here thirteen years I'm still weighing the pluses and the minuses of the move. Waiter service here is not what the First World is used to, but on the other hand, they will never try to push you from the table, even with people waiting. I often eat in the brasserie below my building. One waiter in particular has never been pleasant to me. At a certain lunch and Spanish class, my long-suffering (as long as she has been trying to teach me) tutor Eugenia commented, "I don't think he likes Americans."

Coincidently, when I gave him my order that day, he warned, "That has egg in it."

I am allergic to eggs, and in the thirteen years of eating lunch there on average two times per week, no matter how many times I have mentioned it to the same wait-staff, not once till that day had any of them remembered to warn me. Nope, think again; I tip closer to 15 percent when no Argentine will give more than the customary 10. Nope, I know better than to bark in there. I stood up to shake his hand and say: "Thank you so much for remembering!"

"Well, you have been coming in here for four or five years. I ought to remember."

Correcting, "It will be thirteen years in June."

With little sign of surprise or any other emotion, "Is that so?"

"How long have you been working here?"

"Since nineteen seventy-seven."

I should have figured that one out sooner. Waiters are paid a comparative higher salary and do not rely on tips as heavily as their American counterparts. To fire him, the owner would have to pay him one month's salary for every year he has worked there. By the time of that lunch in May 2015, simple math will tell you he might as well own the place.

Supers of buildings are called *porteros*. They have a strong union, and the same one-month-a-year payoff applies to them as almost all workers in any field. The city is filled with old *porteros* acting like they want to get fired knowing they won't. To get rid of one would require the tenants working together to accomplish it. In this country, that presents a larger problem than Republicans and Democrats compromising for the common good. The upside for service people here, and sometimes both sides in the big picture, is you have to establish relationships with and be kind to workers to hope to get good service. As free enterprising Americans, we often just expect service people to behave like smiling trained seals at the rattling of the change in our pockets. The downside here in Argentina is that if, like me, you are not born into their system, it can be exasperating.

My cousin Steven, his wife, and three kids were coming to visit, so I went to the Teatro Colón to purchase tickets. Sorry, nothing in New York can be compared to it. Think pimped-out La Scala or Bolshoi Theater. At the box office, I asked to buy a whole box for the ballet *Swan Lake* for our group of seven.

The young lady in the box office informed me, "The boxes only have six seats."

I said, "No problema. I'll sit in the neighboring box."

The accommodating young woman smiled and said, "No need for that. The usher can put another seat in there."

She printed out seven tickets all marked for the same box. By theater geography, our seats were right about where Lincoln took it to the head. At the entrance to our box, I handed the twenty-five-something woman our tickets and she informed me, "Only six people are permitted per box."

I replied, "The lady who sold me the tickets said it was okay and that you could bring another chair here."

"I'm sorry, only six people in a box. It's the rule."

"I did not buy these tickets in the street. I bought them at your ticket office downstairs, and all seven tickets denote this box. If that's the rule, why did the lady sell them to me all printed with this box's number on it?" She responded with a blank stare. I asked, "Can you please get your supervisor?"

The short and stout fortyish-looking head usher came over, and we repeated the exact same script as above. I demanded that he take me to see the theater manager. Because I had no plans of backing down, I feared this was to become *Swan Song Lake* for our evening's entertainment. The hard bodies were already twirling and jumping in and out of each other's arms. Not that I cared; we were sitting too far away to give me any thrill. In crept just a little pre-show-two-puff-paranoia, as I feared the agitated usher would be tempted to advance my Lincoln analogy if I got to sit in my desired chair. Eventually, I did something Argentines do far more seldom than New Yorkers and raised my voice. The manager gave the usher a give-the-schnook-his-chair nod and jerky hand signal. Five minutes later, as I had my back to the box entrance, the head usher entered and slammed the chair down on the floor of our box; after the sharp noise ringing in the back of my head, I thought I saw him swinging from a rope onto the stage and shouting, "*Sic semper tyrannis, gringo!*"

What I had failed to recognize then was that what they had tried to pull is an accepted method here for them to get their "gratuity." Showing me that they held the power and extorting the "tip" before the service is just their way. Any time I get in a quagmire with a human obstacle, which is too often, I have to realign my mind-set to understand theirs. They might have got the above backward, just like their grammar, but at least they drive on the correct side of the road.

I was stuck in a traffic jam on a street called Riobamba. I needed to cross a large avenue and a major artery leaving downtown called Cordoba. From my starting point to Cordoba, what normally would take a few minutes had become fifteen. When we finally came to Cordoba, I counted fourteen kids between nine and twelve years old waving signs and blocking traffic that was either trying to turn onto Cordoba or continue on it from the direction of downtown. They were taking pictures of one another with their cell phones, laughing and running around poking one another with their protest signs. There were three police officers protecting them. I could not understand how a country trying to survive in such a competitive world could permit this to happen.

A *porteno* (Buenos Aires native) friend explained it to me this way: "During our dirty war in the late seventies and early eighties, the military government drugged and dropped roughly thirty thousand people into the river. Those people liked to protest in the street, too, albeit a percentage of them also liked to set off bombs. The scars still run deep, so that no organized group—police, politicians, etc.—want to be seen publicly removing people's right to express themselves." *Publicly* is the keyword there, because behind the scenes, they work at it on a full-time basis. A few years ago, the government tried to institute a new law banning books from the United States and Europe because their inks cause cancer. The law did not pass for anything but a message in how far they thought they could go to dupe their public. If I had to think of a good title for the political section of a newspaper here, *Theater of the Absurd* would work. You know how in the United States when people are asked how they are doing, they often answer *Same old, same old?* Argentines don't use that phrase, because it does not apply. Every day is a new adventure.

As a people, if they respect your expert authority at all, it will only last until they feel they can just barely get by without you. It's less about winning as a group and more about the power of the individual. Maybe the banana republic history we thrust on them might have something to do with this. Simply put, they don't want to be subjugated by outsiders.

In New York, every three or four weeks I found someone who might have been telling me the truth. Like for most things, here you wait a little longer. Somewhat understandable when you consider that in many of their lifetimes, telling the truth might have gotten them killed.

Foreigners often find doing business here a death sentence. It's not conducive to business when you mix the above with a people who have no belief in the long term. Why should they? Their populist governments almost as a rule have blown up the economy with hyperinflation and draconian anti-commerce laws enacted to compensate and cover up for their blatant self-interest.

Throughout South America, they are known to be the most arrogant of peoples. I find just the opposite. Most everyone you meet will tell you, "We are a screwed-up people." They are forced to accept systemic corruption because that's what exists here. It is the only system most of them have ever known. Frank Sinatra's song for Buenos Aires might have gone like this: *If you can make it in Buenos Aires, eh, uh . . . Now you're talking!* Frank made two million dollars from his five sold-out performances in Buenos Aires in 1981. His Argentine producer, Enrico Ortega, thanks to the military government and exchange rates, filed for bankruptcy afterward.

Even though they don't see it, they are far, far ahead of us in social skills and good manners. For whatever reason, as a people they appear so much happier than Americans, let alone New Yorkers.

Some stateside friends ask, "Will you ever come home?"

I am.

BROADWAY JOSÉ: LIFE AS A GLADIATOR

My earliest Sundays in memory were spent with my dad and brother watching or listening to the New York Jets. In that era, due to league blackout rules instituted to protect the live gate, home games were only on the radio. Back then if you wanted a higher-definition TV, you sat closer to it. My brother and I would watch the seven road games sitting on the floor a few feet from it.

To date myself as a fan, I went to a "Jets" game in 1961 when they still were the New York Titans and played at the old Polo Grounds. From 1965 and more than a decade forward, the Jets quarterback was Joe Namath (also known as Broadway Joe). He was my first and only sports idol. We had season tickets for two years, ending in 1968, the year before Namath backed up his guarantee and led them to a Super Bowl title. My brother and I alternated going to those games with my dad and his buddy Willie Gilbert. Willie was a successful comedy writer for the stage and television. As we were stuck in the requisite pregame traffic directly in front of Shea Stadium, a twenty something guy in a car filled with them rolled down his window and motioned to Willie to do the same. In the most deadpan voice he could muster, the guy asked Willie a question.

"Excuse me sir, do you know how to get to Shea Stadium from here?"

Willie started to point out the stadium but within a second caught on to the joke and muffled a laugh. Then in lieu of directions, he gave him the wise-guy smirk he had coming. For a few games after that one, in front of the same stadium, Willie asked someone in a neighboring car the exact same stupid question in the same deadpan. Maybe he liked receiving dopey smirks as well as giving them. Another American playwright Clifford Odets said it best: "Mediocrity plagiarizes, geniuses steal boldly." Hanging out with my dad and his buddy, plus the shared experiences like this surrounding the game added to my love for it.

Of all the sports that I played and watched as a youngster in the mid-1960s, football was my clear favorite. At that time in New York's Central Park, Saturday pickup games were easy to find. My older brother and I went looking for them wearing our leather shoulder pads, holding on to our helmets and fantasies of playing at a higher level when we grew up and out. I replayed those games in my mind and daydreamed about the ones to come throughout the following week. As my high school years came around, Mother Nature showed little respect for my football aspirations. Sophomore year she stretched me to all of 5'6" and weighed me in at less than 125 pounds. I came to fear the contact and rode the bench as a point guard in basketball instead of playing quarterback.

After two years of high school and one year of college basketball, I had little more than splinters in my butt to show for my athletic career. I got much better playing in amateur leagues in Houston after college. By then I was 6' tall and was able to compete on close to equal terms with players from Division I schools.

I dreamed about getting a chance to play against those who once bested me. It never happened. I also trained on road bikes with an occasional race. Other than a powerful final sprint (that I was rarely there for), I did not offer much as a competitive cyclist.

In my early forties after the stint in Texas, I moved back to New York. Shortly afterward, I watched the first example of mixed martial arts on television. One skinny Brazilian, Royce Gracie, using submission holds from Brazilian jujitsu, was beating monsters close to 100 pounds heavier than him from various other fighting disciplines. I searched the yellow pages and saw that his cousin, Renzo Gracie, had a school near midtown. I joined and suffered through four months of humiliations before I won my first sparring match. I was hooked. The sport transformed my body and my attitude toward contact and conflict. I added 15 pounds of muscle and carried a lean 195 pounds on my six-foot frame. After two years at the art, in the gym I had beaten a still-active, thirty-year-old ex–All American heavyweight wrestler, a three-time heavyweight US submission grappling champ, and various other people I would never even have dreamed about submitting before learning the sport and the verb in that context. Three years after beginning, at forty-five years old, I won a North American Grappling Association Championship tournament. Not a point was scored against me in my three matches. Disclaimer: There were only seven people in my forty-five-and-older division. It took me that long to find a sport I excelled at. I don't dwell on the fact that hardly anyone practiced it at the time; I won the T-shirt. My natural fear of fighting and violence shifted from getting beaten up to getting sued.

A few years later, I moved to Buenos Aires. I found a car-free circuit to train on my bike, a Brazilian jujitsu school I liked, and enough basketball courts to let me find a game at most times. At a pickup game, I met a young guy from Oregon who worked as a forest firefighter half the year and then traveled the other half. I admired him for following a different path, trying to take in as much of life while he was young. He told me he had read a blurb in the English-language newspaper the *Buenos Aires Herald* about an American football game between Peru and Argentina. We shared a cab.

Peru, having a much greater US influence, had many teams and this one had experienced American coaches. Argentina was in its first year of the tackle version and it showed. Peru already well in the lead tried an on-sides kick in an effort to run up the score. Despite my screaming in broken-play Spanish, they just remained clueless that it was a live ball. None of the Argentine receiving team's front line went for the ball. The Peruvians were taunting our players all over the field and the Argies appeared shell-shocked. It was my second year in Argentina and as well traveled as I was, I had never known a people as warm and welcoming as the Argentines. My early years there were some of the best in my life in almost every way. I loved the people and their country enough to take Peru's bullying personally. I hope that explains away why I called them "our" players and my actions below.

There was no real seating by the field at Club Peron, so I stood on the Argentine sidelines. The wide receiver for Peru was trash-talking at the Argentine cornerback on every play: "You think a punk like you is going to stop me? I'm going to burn your ass, bitch," etc.

Anger got the best of me, leading me to intercede with, "Have your fun now, you scrawny runt. Come back next year and you're gonna get shipped home to your mommy in your duffel bag. That's right, take it, you cowardly trash-squeaking little mutt, I'll be standing right here when the game is over. "

I had learned that the receiver lining up near our sideline was named Hara, so next play: "Hey, Harita la chiquita peruguita, I'm gonna look for you later."

Whoever came my way with a Peruvian uniform got the same and worse. One of the refs was an American assistant coach of

Peru. As he was standing just a few feet from me, my thoughts communicated to him went like this: "You're a real sportsman. The game is brand new here and you're letting your players yelp like the pack of bitches you trained them to be. You're a great ambassador for the sport."

Looking at me, he reached for his flag. I screamed, "Hey I'm just a fan, if I were on this team this bullshit would not be happening."

He looked at the Argentine coach and ordered, "Control your sideline or its going to cost you 15 yards."

A few Argentine players walked over and asked me to cool it. That polite request prompted, "Then one of you give me your freaking helmet. You're the ones that need to be ticked off, cause it's your asses getting abused, not mine. They're humiliating you, you're down more than forty with five minutes to go and you're worried about 15 yards? You shouldn't care about the final score because you're new at this, but it will sting for a long time if you don't try to hit them hard enough to send them home in the belly of the plane while you still got the chance!"

"We are sportsmen in Argentina; we will invite them to drink beer after."

"Do you really think they are worried about advancing the brotherhood of man when they are throwing bombs with the game out of reach? They could care less about being your friends, let alone good sports. They just want to go home and brag how they made you their bitches!"

Not sure how much of my Spanglish rant they understood, but I believe I helped make my point by punctuating my commentary with a bell-ringing slap to one of their helmeted heads. Hardly knowing the individuals or their culture, I was not confident that style of motivation would endear me to them. The Oregonian had been digging my routine, but he had left at halftime to meet a girl. My instincts told me not to count on the Argentines backing me after the game if the Peruvians came over to pass me a case of cleat-borne measles. I thought of leaving early, but as the Argentines I was preaching to had witnessed my challenges to their tormentors, pride obligated me to stay. After the game ended, I did not move from my spot. Two of the Peruvian's line started walking over to me. I glared at them the whole way. It doesn't matter what you know, if two big athletic guys with bad intentions are on your case, you got a problem. As they got close, they extended their hands and said, "Nice game coach." I thought it best not to correct them. I exhaled in the form of a laugh after dodging a hail of Peruvian arrows. I guess I didn't speak Spanglish well enough to ignite their macho.

I don't remember the final score, nor do I want to. I just made sure I got the president of the league's phone number. I felt fully confident that at fifty years old I was in better shape, faster, and stronger than the vast majority of the team. Football-skill-wise it was a no contest. Before going three-quarters insane watching that game, and for the better part of half a century, I had not harbored even the tiniest fantasy of playing organized tackle football.

I called the president of the five-team league and asked him when the next season was starting. He spoke almost no English, my Spanish was at a Pop Warner level. He said there would be a camp for the new recruits starting in a month. He asked me how old I was.

"I'm fifty."

"You want to be a coach?"

"No, I want to play."

"How old are you?"

"I am a very fit fifty."

"Oh, so you want to be a coach."

After a few more go-rounds of the same, I finally got my desire through, and he said he would get back to me after he talked to others involved in the league. After not hearing from him for a week, I called him back. He started, and kept us on the same do-you-want-to-be-a-coach merry-go-round.

Two weeks later I bought a pair of soccer cleats and showed up to camp uninvited. I found my phone friend the president standing with chairman Gustavo. The president was a tall, thin guy sporting a mustache in the style of a baseball player from the 1920s. He appeared a little taken aback that I had invited myself. Gustavo Rodriguez was a clean-shaven, rock-hard 215 pounds on a 5'9" frame. Gustavo seemed a little more welcoming, maybe because he had his eyes on the books and saw me as another paying customer. Neither was directly affiliated with any team. The two were part of a larger group that ran things. I told them I had my own health insurance and would sign any waiver they put in front of me. I think they gave me the okay out of curiosity more than any other reason.

The camp coaching staff was close to worthless as far as teaching football fundamentals. That wasn't their apparent intention anyways. It was nothing more than a fraternity hazing, trying to make people quit who were not willing to take their abuse in the hydration-deprived, six-hour practices. As a by-product of their dangerous methodology, they were hoping for a little Stockholm syndrome effect to garner loyalty down the road. Anytime they screamed at me, I could not hold back a smile. I guess they let me get away with it due to my age. When not at the Saturday and Sunday camp, I had my 240-pound Brazilian jujitsu instructor try to hold me back from pushing him across the room for half an hour after class.

Between that and cycling with a peloton of high-level master racers, I felt as fit as I ever had been. I prayed for the first day of contact. I was also a little nervous, as it was something I was intimidated by in what felt like a past life. When the day came to put on the pads, I wished it could have never ended. I hit so fearlessly, it was as if I were making up for all my past self-perceived cowardice.

It didn't matter if it was a friend made during camp or how big they were, I went to destroy whoever they put in front of me.

During the fifth week, they had a combine to test the player's athletic skills. Out of twenty-six, I finished third, with fifty legit push-ups, near the middle in the 40-yard dash even after stumbling in a small hole. Overall, I was in the top third.

The last practice of the six-week camp, they made each player run a gauntlet of sorts. Four of the coaching staff who were also players suited up and made you run through them, while they threw cheap shots from all angles. As I watched the preceding victims, I formulated a plan and then executed it this way: I was given the ball about ten yards from them. I charged at them as hard as I could. When I got within a few feet, I stopped abruptly and softly lobbed the ball above the head of the first player on my left. As he reached up for it, I drilled my shoulder into his sternum, knocking enough of his wind out to remove him from the battle. I turned to the player on my right and scraped the arch of my cleat down his ankle planting it on his foot, then pushed him over. The third guy and I blocked each other a few times, and as I saw the fourth coming, I dove for his knees and tackled him. I jumped back to my feet quickly. He was still on all fours with his back to me. I swung my leg far enough back to kick his ass through the uprights from 59 yards out. Near the point of contact, I put the brakes on and just used my cleated shoe to push him flat. I remember them all crashing their helmets into mine, turning that ill-fitting piece of junk sideways on my head. I was pouring blood from my chin, sucking for air, and throwing body punches at whoever was in front of me. I made my point: *F you and your bullshit camp, and I am not here to take abuse but to give it.*

For draft day they rented a restaurant and copied the NFL draft as best they could. It was a suit-and-tie affair with family and friends invited. There was a projector to put up a composite picture of each player, including physical stats and projected position, as he got selected. I thought I made a better impression than to have been drafted thirteenth of twenty-sixth as a linebacker, especially after showing I was the only one of the bunch who could complete a pass. I rationalized, maybe teams did not see me as a long-term prospect. After only experiencing tackle-football seated on my couch for close to forty years, I was still thrilled to be living this dream. The Gladiators selected me after two twenty-seven-year-old players, a German-born and mostly Argentine-raised 5'11" receiver named Raul. He lacked a little toughening up, yet athletic wise clearly deserved his first-round selection. The second pick was a monster lineman from Denmark. We all hit it off from the start.

The coach was not a player but had been one in Panama, where there are several leagues. Although ours was an amateur league, the guy stuck with organizing each team was called the owner. Manuel was our "owner." He was a thirty-three-year-old labor leader who had the gift of gab. I found him entertaining, even if half his rap seemed invented and filled with secret agendas. He spoke English, as his father's company had sent them to Great Britain for three years while he was in high school.

Eight days after the draft the league had a skill-assessment practice with all the teams. I was the only rookie who went over to the quarterback section. It consisted of nothing more than throwing bombs to receivers on fly routes. I threw the ball an easy fifteen yards farther and completed at double the rate of the next best QB. I ran over to Manuel two times to ask him to bring the coach over to watch me dismantle the competition. He yeah, yeah'd me both times, but the coach never came.

During the Gladiators' first team practice, Manuel told me, "The coach does not want a quarterback who can't speak Spanish perfectly; communication is fundamental in football."

Manuel and another guy were the quarterbacks. Not a tough communiqué to decipher. Manuel was slow a foot and could barely throw the ball more than 25 yards. The other guy was athletic, had a slightly better arm, with zero football instincts. For instance, as he was running out of bounds he once panic-tossed the ball un-derhanded to a defenseman a few feet in front of him as if he were color-blind or it was an early Christmas present.

For the first two preseason games, I was on the kicking teams and the defensive line. On a kickoff-receiving team, I ran into one of the opposition who didn't see me coming. Ka-boom, sent him flying. One more thing checked off the list of things I wanted to experience in life. I would have used the clichéd term *bucket list*, but channeling my inner Joe Namath, the room left in that almost bottomless pail is reserved for other types of adventures. It's not as if I didn't enjoy being a lineman, but as my interest was in win-ning football games, I was frustrated by not playing at my natural position of quarterback, especially as there was no one else on the team that could even fake it. We lost both preseason games. We lost our first real game also. At a practice after that defeat, Manuel and the head coach were absent. I asked the defensive coach and skilled Panamanian linebacker Santiago if I could take a turn at QB; he said sure. Besides Manuel, Santiago was the only player to have the coach's ear. After the following practice with the coach, Santiago's discovery became the new starting quarterback.

The following game was with the Aguilas, who with a few ex-ceptions were mediocre. One and a half of those exceptions was an interior lineman named Juan. He was both exceptionally wide and fast. Juan rarely found anybody between us who could stop his 250 pounds from landing on top of me. Other than Manuel, now a tight end, and Raul, the rookie wide out, none of our re-ceivers would run a complete route. No matter how many times I explained it, they would stop and wait for me to throw them the ball to a spot they picked out all on their own. I played pretty ner-vous and did not have a good grasp of the plays. I would rate my play a D. We lost, and they went back to the old QB. We lost the next game also. The following game was against the 3-0 Lobos, who had the biggest line in the league. I had watched the Lobos play the Stallions in the second week of the season. In that game, the noise was deafening, they left no doubt that they were the two hardest-hitting teams.

While playing, I enjoyed trying to Zen through the noise of the crashing pads. Those sounds are a big part of what sells the game. Concussions could be eliminated if all helmets were soft and inflated with enough air. Except instead of appearing like the Roman-gladiator spectacle it now resembles, it would look and sound like Son of Flubber or kids bouncing around in an inflatable McDonald's fun house. Think of bowling without the noise of the pins crashing.

From the sidelines, the decibel level caused by the contact had me cringing. I speculated as to how my now fifty-one-year-old, skinny-legged Jew self would hold up in all that chaotic violence. Creeping into my thoughts was, *Maybe exercising discretion later in life is not cowardice but the smart thing.* At the same time, I was proud that I was testing myself at something I had wimped out on earlier on. From a lifespan timeline perspective, my athletic career was happening in reverse.

The other QB didn't show up to the game. By default I was back in there. It was a blessing that I didn't know beforehand I was starting. Consequently, I didn't psyche myself up all week and come overly pumped to the game. I jogged onto the field more relaxed and cerebral. The plays came in from the sidelines. If the pass was not to Manuel or Raul, I looked downfield with little intention of throwing it. I would tuck it and run. If the play sent in was a triple reverse on our own twenty to "help run out the clock for the first half," I pretended to miss the initial handoff and ran it with both hands on the ball. After watching the Lobos two weeks earlier, oddly I felt let down that their shots didn't hurt worse. I quickly gained the confidence that I could do anything I wanted out there. Their defense was too spread apart, and they were slow to react to my decisions to fake a pass and then run. For the first time, I had filtered out all extraneous thoughts and only concentrated on the game. I couldn't even hear the noise of the pads. In one sense, playing quarterback held the most relaxing moments of my life. I had not a millisecond to fret over the normal menu of problems that weighed on me, but only time to focus on executing the play. Freeing your mind is an unheralded pleasure of being "in the zone."

At halftime we were up fourteen to nothing, and the team was celebrating as if the game had ended that way. I felt the need to remind them, "Hey, guys, this game isn't over; we celebrate after, not now. Now we concentrate on how to give them a worse beating the coming half than the last one. We really need to kick these clowns hard now that we have them down." So as not to scream *I am claiming leadership* just yet, I lightened it up with, "One of you clowns get on the ground and I'll show you how it's done."

Another reason I tried to entertain them was to distract them from any lingering fears they might be having; I wanted them to play like they were ready to die for the cause. I rushed for 68 yards on seven attempts, including a touchdown, and went four for six on my passes, with one going for a score to Raul. We won 26-10. It was far and away the biggest upset in league history. After the game, we shared a larger and more joyous camaraderie than I had ever experienced on any team.

That night my girlfriend and I went to a restaurant a block from the house to celebrate. By the end of dinner, I could not get out of the chair on my own. At home that evening, I noticed both of my hips were black, blue, purple, and various shades of yellow the size of a helmet in circumference. I learned to enjoy leaving the games feeling great and then lie in bed at night trying to figure out which hit wrought each painful bruise as they popped up one by one.

There was a four-week break to savor the victory as the all-star team was preparing to play Paraguay. I went to the try outs for that team. In my first huddle as QB, a few players from other teams gave me lip. "Speak Spanish; we can't understand you. Pay attention to the coach." Etc. The only reason I didn't freak out on them in that circle of contempt was that I thought it would kill my chances to make the team. I completed the three passes I attempted. On one rifled short completion over the middle, the twenty-five-year-old Peruvian coach stopped play to demonstrate how I should throw that pass higher and softer. I didn't even have time to take my helmet off to scratch my head on that piece of advice. I got cut. The guy they selected as the starter was the pay-attention-to-the-coach instigator. He couldn't run and couldn't throw the ball more than 30 yards compared to my 50. The playbook consisted of six back-field-busy run plays and three pass plays instituted by our coach. He did not have one basic running play in the scheme. This coach played for the Stallions, who had four other Peruvian players, including the guy whose backside I booted in the camp's gauntlet. When not trying to exert his authority, he sat on the bench snuggled up to Gustavo, a power on the league's board. They lost that game to a country of seven million that had only two teams. They were now 0 and 2 against Paraguay.

The other thing that stuck in my craw about the Peruvian coach/cornerback/quarterback was this: Before games, the league would divide up the equipment between the two teams. In a pre-season game against his team, he ran over to me and told me that the helmet that was placed on our sideline and that I had selected was really his property.

I asked him, "How and why did the league put your personal helmet on our side?"

With a sad puppy face, "I don't know."

Rather than walk the helmet over to someone for confirmation, I took his word for it. He played with it, and I wore a helmet that spun on my head *Exorcist*-style. I later learned, as I had suspected, that it was not his helmet. It was after that game that I

13

had a friend coming down to visit bring a pro-level helmet and quarterback shoulder pads. There were two games per Saturday, if the helmet con artist and I were not playing against each other, he would ask to borrow my shoulder pads. I never once declined or even brought up his prior helmet trickery. Amongst a certain type of people, altruistic behavior does not bring you respect or appreciation, but rather a laugh behind your back at your weakness and stupidity.

Most of the Gladiators would come over to my apartment on Sundays, as I had the DIRECTV NFL football package—and equally as inviting, my domestic employee, Marta, made a *guiso* (stew). They were all so nice, and nobody came empty-handed. I felt lucky to be part of this team. I'd been on a lot of teams, and this one was the tightest. Once the beer started flowing, it became open season on everybody. Our fullback's weight, my age, Rafael's ability to down half a quart of Vodka were all roasted in the target-rich environment of my TV room.

They perennially pleaded with me to put on my obnoxious New York accent and attitude. "Okay, you jerkoffs, who is it the F that you think that you lowlifes are, to tell me, of all peoplez, how to speak. Just be happy I speak the language of the First World." I typically finished with, "Remember, there is no *I* in team, but there is in Michael." I think everyone in that room thought of the others as family of sorts. I always tried to get Manuel to come, as I feared my own increasing popularity for political reasons. He had family obligations and only showed up once.

I respected the coach, because he took the job seriously and came to the games prepared. He enjoyed the victories more than anybody and took the losses the hardest. He put a lot of time and effort into it. I thought he was a good leader, and I liked him. From a strategic standpoint, he lacked at that point in his coaching career. It's a lot of responsibility to manage a game as just one person, even if you have a lot of experience. Still, he handled it well. Despite my increasing frustrations with strategy and the play-calling, I thought it more important not to challenge his authority in any way, for the team's benefit. Almost every time rookie Raul was at my house and had my attention alone, he would gas me up how I should be the coach. I explained to him that we are all learning and we will all get better as the season goes on, including the coach. Raul defines himself as a lot of things, one being a *revolutionary.* He struck me as a little lost, with few friends. He spent a good deal of time at my house, as he had a real love for the game and liked to watch it with me. He seemingly lived to discuss tactics and hear my opinions on the plays we viewed. He was interesting and enthusiastic; my girlfriend had no problem with his coming for almost all the televised games, including Monday night football.

The five team's owners and Gustavo had a single vote in the league decisions with the president having two. Politics played a big part of everything. After the national team game against Paraguay, Manuel who was often the swing vote between the president and his rival, Gustavo, finagled his way into bringing a friend of his who was a quarterback in the flag football league for a mid-season tryout. I asked Manuel why I had to go to a six-week camp and this new guy did not.

"Because he has a lot of experience."

"Where did he get this experience?"

"In the flag football league."

"I was the quarterback for my flag football league in college for three years. I was a starting quarterback on my prep school tackle intramural team for the only year I was there."

"Well your experience was a long time ago."

"Okay, Manuel, if you and coach think he can help the team, I'm all for it."

With the offensive line and the play-calling as they were, I tried to convince myself that it might even come as a relief to play another position. I had asked the coach earlier if we could settle on one center instead of the three he rotated. I believed it would cut down on fumbles between the center, QB exchange. I got a no. I tried another tack and asked the coach if we could run some of the plays out of the shotgun formation, humbly disguising it with "because I'm a little slow to get back." After the tone of that no, I didn't bother trying to lend my ideas to the coach. Manuel's great beige hope looked good in that practice, in spite of my friends testing his toughness in a big way. Maybe it was in too big of a way, because he never came to another practice. I was the starting quarterback from then on, although I often got yanked midgame after a bad play or what the coach considered a bad play on my part. After the fifth game I didn't bother to try to enlist Manuel's help with my frustrations or ideas. He had continually and passionately agreed with me, but the only solutions I figured he actually tried to put across to the coach were trying to convince him that he should be the quarterback and, when that failed, trying to place his "experienced" friend as the quarterback. When I relayed my level of exasperation as a result of the absurdities I was dealing with to a friend in the States, he, with sympathetic frustration, told me to ask the coach "Are you interested in winning?" Clearly my buddy had never lived in South America. If he had, he would have understood that winning as a team is secondary to having the complete power and control to assert your self-interest. Hmm, well maybe let's not limit that to South America.

I tried not to show it, but I leaned toward the president in the power struggle for the league control for various reasons. To start with, he was more presentable in an executive way than Gustavo. He also spoke of his plans to grow the sport here. In one game were our coach had walked off in frustration, we were down five points with only enough time on the clock for our kickoff return. I took control and inserted myself onto the return team to start the desperation trick play I had set up. They would lateral it to me, and

I would throw it a little backward across the field to our fastest guy. It did not work, but what I recall most about that play was what my girlfriend told me she had overheard. Gustavo was riding the guy I took out on the sidelines: "Are you going to let that *gringo* tell you what to do? He's not the coach; he can't yank you out of the game." If I had thought about it, I would have asked for a volunteer to sit out, but in the heat of battle that's how it went. Obviously, my lack of democratic etiquette is not why I remember that play.

The last game of the season was against the defending champs, the Toros. They were short-handed, but still it was our best game of the year; we blew them out 44-6. I hit Raul twice for touchdowns. One of the TDs I later enjoyed watching more than any pass I had thrown to date for the following reason: The tape showed me doing something I rarely remember doing—scanning the field and then looking back to Raul before hitting him. If I have misled led you to this point as far as the skill level involved here, apologies. Think small-town junior varsity. Hitting-wise it was another story; I'll get to my surgeries later.

After the first season, the president told me he received a call from Football USA (the blanket organization for all levels of football in the States) inviting him and one other person from Argentina to a meeting in Orlando to help organize and promote football in Latin America. Football USA would pay the hotel, but the two invitees had to pay for their own flights. The president was not sure he had the money to go and would need a translator even if he came up with the cash. He figured nobody else would have the funds to go either. I offered, "If the league agrees, I'll pay for both of our flights as a donation to the league, and I'll be your translator." He said he would check it out with the others.

In the meantime, I had a phone conversation with a honcho from Football USA. He was the guy that South America would answer to if he could get the teams on the continent organized. The guy loved my stories, especially the one about a certain team's tight end coming to a game intoxicated. The player had been used to shuttle in the plays. Drunk, he was still better than the next guy, so they played him. As the second half began, the coach was screaming for him to come over to get the next play to bring in. He stayed seated on his helmet and laughingly proclaimed, "Your FedEx man is on strike." Despite everyone's crazed encouragements, he continued to sit on his helmet as if trying to hatch it. He looked up toward the sky smiling and drinking what all hoped was only Gatorade.

The Football USA guy was jovial and sounded like he was eating a sandwich both times I talked to him. We hit it off, and in the second conversation, he asked, "Why don't you run South America as our liaison? The guy in Chile doesn't speak English, and I don't trust the guy in Mexico."

I informed him, "Chile has a little-brother complex with Argentina, and I don't think any of the countries will take too kindly to a North American transplant being the South American representative. I would be more than happy to help you any way you think I can in a nonofficial capacity."

We expressed our desire to meet each other at the meeting. I would have loved the job, but I didn't want Gustavo or the president to think I was trying an end-run around them. I was thankful to be playing and wanted nothing more than to help them in this instance. I called both to recount the conversations with Football USA so as to let them know they were in the driver's seat to run the show in Latin America.

A few days later, I asked the president if the league had approved my donation and me going along with him to Orlando. "Sorry, you can't go, but they will accept your donation. They don't know who but they are going to send one of the team owners along with me."

Oh, how nice of them!

I was relieved not to have to come out of pocket for the two tickets. A few days after I snuffed out that idea, the president called me to confide in me that "the league never had any intention of sending anyone else; the others just wanted to show you they had that power over you. You can go now and your donation is expected."

I replied, "I got invited to go to a dance, then got uninvited, and now I am reinvited because they find my wallet irresistible. Me and my hurt feelings decline." *Now go answer to French Guiana for all your football needs.*

I only yelled at my offensive line once the whole year. I never blamed any of the centers for the fumbles between us. I told them this: I don't care where on your ass you snap it, just keep snapping it to the same place. We finished the season 4 and 4. I worked hard at trying to believe that if we recruited well and had a decent draft we could be a lot better team next year.

During an off-season workout, we played a game of touch football. You could only get one first down and that was marked by shirts on both sides of the imaginary 50 yard line. Salvador, Manuel's best friend on the team was the referee. I was covering Manuel on a completed sideline play. It was their 4th down. I played off of him because I timed it so that I would tag him a few yards before the marker, which I clearly did. Obviously, they turned it over on downs, our ball. Salvador signaled it was a 1st down.

I looked at Salvador incredulously, pointed to the 1st down marker, and said, "You were standing right there; the marker is right in front of you. How could you call that a 1st down?"

He said nothing; I kept up questioning him as he fought to keep a straight face. It finally dawned on me that it was nothing more than a blatant cheat for his buddy. *Okay, Salvador, my mistake. Please forgive me. Being I am from the Northern Hemisphere, I got things upside down and backward. With my confused gravity, every other time I try to stand up straight my head goes up my ass, and then even after I yank it out, I still can't see because I'm tea-bagging myself.* Both were also referees for the league. In at least one sense, I was grateful these two "politicians" were on my team. In another sense, from that moment on I could not stand the presence of the brazen cheater Salvador.

A few days later the majority of the team went to a club on the outskirts of town. I rode in Manuel's car with his buddy Salvador and two others. On the way back, Salvador could not stop puking out of the front passenger window. I was sitting in the back with the window sealed shut. In spite of the difficulty in watching someone vomit, I enjoyed each upchuck more than the last. In the middle of an episode, I asked, "Hey, the other day when you called Manuel's catch a 1st down, where you this drunk also?" To be sure he heard the question, I repeated it the second his head came back in the window. "Hey, Salvador, do you want to finish my ham and cheese sandwich; it's got too much mayo on it for me?" The idea of someone busting my balls when that sick would have me seeking revenge in ways I could not put in writing. What goes around just came around.

VIVA LOS VIKINGOS!

The president called me to go have a beer with him and Manuel. He got right to their proposal. "The league wants a sixth team and chose you to start it as the 'owner.' "

I hesitated, then while looking at Manuel told them, "Thanks, but I really feel like I'm part of the Gladiators; I have a lot of good friends on the team."

Manuel began the sales pitch with, "Most of the players have friends on other teams, and it's not going to stop me from being friends with you." . . . You fill in the cliché . . .

"Isn't there someone else who wants their own team; how about the coach?"

The president replied, "The coach wanted it, but we feel he is entrenched in the Gladiators and you have the wherewithal to get it started.

Other than having a few dollars in my pocket, what did I do wrong to not get considered entrenched? In other words, I was going to have to order and pay for the new uniforms to have them in time for the season.

As I was reading the writing of their playbook on the wall, I feebly offered back, "Where would I even get the players from?" We played nine-man football because our field was narrower than regulation. Even so, you could not expect to compete with less than fifteen or sixteen players. Guys would have the occasional family or work obligations. Injuries come with the territory, and now and then players would stay out clubbing too late Friday night to show up Saturday. Three of the teams had close to twenty; the other two looked like Ohio State on the sidelines.

The president offered this deal: "You will get the first pick in the draft. On top of that, you can select one player from each team and they can only protect three players." I calculated that that might add up to at most nine players. I would have to recruit the rest on my own. Each team was only allowed six foreigners.

"Let me get back with you guys tomorrow, or the next day." At home, the more I thought of how enthusiastic a salesman Manuel was in that meeting, the more I realized *adios* would have a big upside. As I considered another season with him running things, the more I wanted out. Once I decided starting a new team was my only real option if I wanted to play real football, my heart began to break. I hated the thought of leaving my buddies on the Gladiators and did not know how I would muster the strength to tell them. When I did, I threw it on the league and Manuel. I certainly wasn't going to protect him from the truth. His year-long barrage of double-talk had my head spinning harder than any hit I took all that season. The league guys weren't all that well liked or respected, and the truth was this was their idea. Sure, I could have said no, but everything pointed to them putting "incumbent" next to QB and my name on the roster.

One of the linemen who looked up to me felt so betrayed that he has not spoken to me since the day he heard that news. I was moved by the players' emotions my exit brought forth. Their sentiments had me feeling like I let myself get roped into a huge blunder that would cause me to lose the best friends I had made in Argentina. I felt like I was the front-runner for the Benedict Arnold trophy, awarded to the player who dicks his buddies the hardest. On the other hand, it was as if three sets of water-logged shoulder pads were lifted off of me. I was now in a position to build and run a team the way I felt it should be. Not that I was really too sure of the *how it should be* part.

Raul and the Dane came over to my apartment to discuss their football futures. The Dane was the best offensive lineman in the league and was also good on the defensive side. Raul did toughen up and had improved greatly over the year. He was now a valuable receiver and cornerback. We were all close, and they were the most regular visitors at my house. They knew football well enough to know they wanted off the Gladiators too, and saw me as their ticket out. I came up with a plan. They would bluff Manuel and the coach into believing that if they were not traded to my new Vikingos, they were done with Fútbol Americano. Manuel immediately smelled me out as the rat behind this. As part of the ruse when he called, I got my sanctimonious on:

"They are your players, and I will not accept them under any circumstances. Letting them circumvent the rules would create anarchy, and I told them both that."

Manuel relayed that to Raul and the Dane and they responded with, "Okay, fine, F you and F Mike. We're not playing next year."

If they weren't going to play football, Broadway and Hollywood awaited them. Two weeks later Manuel, now sold on their act and trying to salvage something for them, "convinced" me to take them for a second- and third-round pick. After two years in the league, you're allowed to declare yourself a free agent and play for whomever you want, as long as they accept you. The two, of course, only had the one year in the league.

The Lobos had three malcontents who wanted out of that wolf pack. They also all had only one year in the league. One was the

QB of the National team and a tough-as-nails linebacker. The other two were solid players at this level. The QB was the guy who barked at me the loudest in the huddle when I was taking my turn at quarterback during the National team tryouts. I thought about that subterfuge, and all the stories I had heard about them through the Malbec grapevine, when they approached me about joining the new Vikingos. The trio had played together in the flag football league; they were all around thirty years old. I feared this cleated triumvirate could be dangerous to the seedling that was my team. They told me that Gustavo had given them the unconditional okay to play wherever they wanted. They were good, and at that moment, including myself, I had all of three players.

In spite of my trepidations, I called the QB guy back and told him, "I would love to have you guys. I don't care what anybody on that team says about you. You will be on a new team with a new start and a clean slate. If I am the coach and we are competing for the QB position, we can discuss how the selection is made beforehand, but after that, we will have nothing to say about it other than with our play. If I were to use my influence to get that position in any way, I believe we would become a political group rather than a winning football team."

He could not have sounded happier. I felt large listening to my own moral and magnanimous speech, even if I wasn't sure how much I meant it.

A few days later, I got a call from Gustavo asking me if I had taken those players on to my new team. I said yes, but only after they had told me you had given them permission to come over. He began his speech: "It would be detrimental to the league if players had the power to abandon their teams without following the rules and play wherever they felt like it."

"I agree and know the rule. The only reason I accepted them is because they had assured me that you had given them the okay to leave that team beforehand."

"Well, like I said, it would not be good for the league."

I did not press him about whether he had given them permission as he continued on about how management needs to stick together, etc. My mistake; I should have called Gustavo for confirmation. I phoned the QB guy back: "I'm sorry but I cannot take you guys." I didn't offer an explanation, as I felt it best I take the bullet for Gustavo even though I assumed he had misled them. I can't imagine the three of them had a hard time figuring it out. They ended up getting traded to the Aguilas, who at least had enough players to compensate for them.

On a Sunday, Raul and the big Dane came over to watch football and talk about recruiting. It was eerie without all the other guys cramming into the TV room. Instead of sitting by ourselves, we went to Casa Bar, a sports bar not far from the house. It was close to packed. We spotted a table for four that had a guy with a Mets hat sitting by himself; he invited us to join him. We introduced ourselves and shortly thereafter we learned that our new twenty-seven-year-old friend Greg had moved down here from Connecticut to open up a software company. I told him the story of our starting a new team in the league, which he had not known about. He told us that he had played Division I football as a wide receiver for Duke. Raul, the Dane, and I looked at one another as if just discovering we shared a winning lottery ticket.

"Greg, let me be as subtle as I can; your fate has been decided. As the Grand High Ruler of the American football team the Vikingos, I have this to say: First off, from this day forward, you do not pay for your own beers. Second, you are now appointed head coach and soon-to-be-most-valuable player of the Vikingos."

He laughed and said he would play but wouldn't have time to coach. The next day, Greg (also known as The Big G) and I went to a school's field to throw it around. He was fast, as in faster than anyone in the league who weighed over 150 pounds. He caught everything that came remotely close to him. He was impressed enough with my arm. He sailed a pass over my head in the direction of the school. I stopped and turned around and told him, "Sorry I can't go get that ball."

"Why not?"

"That would put me within 300 yards of the school, and the terms of my probation state that's a no-no." He cracked up and we became fast friends.

I hooked up with Raul to help figure out which players from the other teams we wanted. He knew the other team's players better than me. I only loved football; he lived for it. Raul was also a fair judge of talent. Afterward, I called Manuel to give him my choices. He informed me, "We changed a few things and you are still going to get one player from each team. But each team will choose who they'll give."

"Manuel, that wasn't the deal we made. Now I'm going to get players who don't show up to practice or games, and if they do, I'm probably going to wish they hadn't."

"Sorry, that was a league decision."

All five team's records were fairly close, and each game was normally tough. I slowly figured out that they were looking for a patsy to pad their records, and all the better if the wins came against an American beat at his own game.

━◆ ◆━

I took an ad out in the *Buenos Aires Herald* and *La Nación*:

> *Fútbol Americano. Positions open: Hostile and violence-prone individuals preferred. Size and speed help but not a prerequisite. Social skills not required.*

The first call generated by the *Herald* ad was from an American insurance guy who was here indefinitely. Over the phone Stewart told me he had played tight end at Miami of Ohio; I was impressed and breathed a sigh of relief to be moving in the right direction. I went to meet the guy at his spacious office overlooking the city in the high-dollar enclave of Recoleta. Our long conversation made me feel like I was on an interview-gone-bad to work for him. There were pictures of my prospect on various racing sailboats on the walls. He was a portly thirty-one-year-old. A tall, out-of-shape Rudy came to mind. He mentioned he wasn't sure how his leg would hold up. That prompted a long-winded story of his knee having been shattered while jumping from his boat into a smaller one. I was bored to the point of not being able to stop repeating in my head, *Dinged being mutinied off into a dinghy.*

He did a fair amount of traveling for his job. Regardless, I was so busy trying to get this team off the ground that to snare him I offered Stewart the added title of Head Coach. He bit, and I had another skilled player. He was off on various business trips when most of the players were arriving on the scene. Thus, Raul, Greg, and I were making the decisions.

Rodrigo (renamed Arnold by Greg after a soon-to-be-described infamous event) was the first to answer the ad I placed in *La Nación*. He was a tall and speedy twenty-five-year-old Argentine. He had no football experience but had run track. He assured us he was not afraid of contact. Arnold had just returned from living in Austria for three years. Immediately I assumed he had learned something about organization and punctuality after staying in a country that is a lot more famous for those things than his own. The big G and I met him, and we both found him humble and reserved yet with a little something about him that hinted if there was fun to be had, he would be there. Special teams and cornerback is what we figured him for.

Again from *La Nación* came Miguel. He was also an Argentine speedster who had fallen in love with the niche sport of Fútbol Americano from watching a few games a year on television. Miguel was another easygoing personality who took to hitting like he was born to it. Special teams and linebacker is where Greg figured he fit. I thought he had potential as a running back. Even after advertising for pricks, we came up with a lot of nice guys for this team. As far as personalities go, Miguel and Rodrigo (without them saying much) were two of my favorites. The typical Argentine personality is as close to perfect as I have met in all my travels. They are polite to a fault, are non-confrontational, and have etiquette in areas where we North Americans never learned we needed it. They are warm, engaging, and curious about you. They drink to excess less often than we do. If you have associated with enough people who do, it should explain why I digressed.

One of the all-around dirtiest players to show up was a Chilean in his late twenties named Esteban. He was a fund-raiser for a charitable organization. I could understand why he was a natural at it, because everyone bought his story of humble beginnings—even after hearing various versions of it. He dressed casual but in designer brands. He was about 5'10", was 200 pounds, and had played in Chilean leagues for years. He told us he was a quarterback; after seeing him throw a few knuckleballs and then comparing that to watching him hit, we slotted him in at linebacker/fullback and third-string QB behind me and Greg.

With, Esteban, Stewart, the Dane, Greg, Raul, and myself, I was at the allotted limit for foreigners when I got a call from a nineteen-year-old Canadian farm boy's girlfriend. She was studying abroad and was looking for something to keep Homer busy during the days. She set up the meeting, and I went to talk to him at his hostel. He came down to the crowded bar naked except for a small towel around his waist. I was taken aback at his decision to show up to a meeting in a public space practically

naked, but when I remembered what I had in store for his 6'2"
and 220 pounds of no-fat farm strength, I was taken forward in a
big way. He claimed he was a high school star and was recruited
by Magill University. If that were true, it would say more about
Magill's scholastic enrollment guidelines than anything else. He
did not strike me as sharp. The next day we went to a park. After
watching son of Gump run, I decided then and there that if the
league would not make an exception for Homer, I would become
the water boy to clear a space for him. The top four of the now
six teams would make the play-offs. The Canuk was only going
to be around for six of the games before returning to Canada. I
figured even playing just that many of the ten-game schedule, he
was my meal ticket into the play-offs.

I met Manuel the next day and told him, "The season is right
around the corner, and I only have seven players. Do you think the
league can make an exception, as I might have another foreigner?
He's only going to be here for the first half of the season anyhow."

He asked, "Is he big?"

"I just met him briefly, and he appeared maybe just a little
above average to me."

"Is he fast?"

Hunching my shoulders with hands out and palms up, "Uh,
I dunno, never seen him run. He's a Canuk, put him on a pair
of hockey skates and I'm sure he can move. Manuel, why are you
asking? If I were to tell you he is short, fat, and slow, would that
improve my chances? I've got seven guys so far. Do you want to
see me get killed out there? I didn't sign up for this to die in the
process. Do you expect us to make it through a season with eleven
or twelve players? We'll have to forfeit half our games. I've already
been screwed big-time about the players the other teams were supposed to give up. First I was supposed to pick anyone except all but
three protected players per team; then it changed to whoever they
chose, and now they're all balking at even that. They're crying,

'It will hurt our team dynamics,' but what about my ass's welfare dynamics?"

I joined Raul and the Dane as Academy Award nominees. Manuel helped clear the way for the extra foreigner. His team, the Gladiators, had almost thirty in uniform and gave us two from the end of the bench that wanted out, Martino and Ivan. Martino was a fireman, and an undersized lineman. He was an all-around good guy and, more important, fearless. He was the third-string center and of the three I played with on the Gladiators, I liked him the best. He had a willingness to hit, be hit, and learn. Ivan was a schoolteacher, approaching forty, fair-sized, but nobody would describe him as athletic. Pick any high school in the United States and the jocks would've picked on him, too brainy. He seemed so happy to be part of this new team and showed the heart and loyalty of a stray dog that had finally found a loving home.

The last guy to answer the *Nación* ad was Jeraldo. He was a forty-four-year-old rugby player standing all of about 5'8". Now for the good parts: he was 210 pounds of pure muscle and as fast as Homer in the 40-yard dash. For the best part, he was the head bouncer for one of the most famous strip bars in town. Even if he possessed none of the described physical assets, he would likely be considered Most Valuable Teammate.

The camp for the rookies was nearing its completion. Raul and I were fixtures there observing the talent. I hope people at the camp got a kick out of my imitation of Jerry Lewis's dad in the movie *That's My Boy*; for sure, I did. Every time Miguel made a good play, I moved my head side to side with a swagger looking for eye contact with all close to me, as I repeated in the same dopey-proud voice of the actor, "That's my Boy, that's my boy." This wasn't France, so no one knew that I clipped the line.

SHE CAN PLAY CENTER FOR ME ANYTIME

S tewart, our new coach, had been excused from the torture of the league's camp sessions, as he had college experience. He never showed up to one to observe the talent. A few days before the draft, Raul came over to my apartment to discuss selection strategies. He had put all the pluses and minuses of each potential pick on a separate piece of paper and laid them out on my dining room table. We moved them around simulating various potential draft scenarios. I was so impressed by Raul's work that I appointed him team president on the spot. I was even more thrilled than him. If you were sentenced to attending a few league meetings, you would know why. I had some fear that the master manipulator of discord, Gustavo, would try to put him on an "Amway High" by convincing him that it should, and could, be his team. Raul came back from his first league meeting singing Gustavo's praises. I made Raul understand that I had no personal problem with Gustavo. I respected the work he put in, but so far the president had been the only one to not go out of his way to screw us.

I saw a sale on sets of hip, knee, and quadriceps pads on a US website. I decided to make a donation to the league, as they were short on these items. I bought twenty sets for three hundred dollars. I had to go out to customs at the airport—a half a day of waiting in lines later and an additional three hundred dollars for five days of storage. At that time, I could have paid a garage in the most expensive neighborhood to park a car for six months for less. I proudly handed them to the league. Gustavo purportedly doubled the price per set once again and sold them. A year later the president said he never saw them accounted for in the books. Around the time of my donation, Gustavo found himself on the outside of a mining business he had inherited a piece of and began work as a waiter. If the league never saw the cash, to date that is the largest tip I have ever given.

I got a call from the host of sports program that had read my advertisement. His channel is seen all over South America. "We would like to interview you about starting this new league."

I corrected, "I did not form the league, just the new team, the Vikingos."

He said, "Okay, then we would like to interview you about your new team."

In consideration of Gustavo's and the president's efforts in running the league, I told the interviewer, "I would suggest you call Gustavo. He is one of the head honchos in the league and is a native Spanish Speaker."

I really wanted to stutter through the interview but thought it would serve me best to not look like I was stealing anyone's thunder in this arena. In spite of knowing that exposure could help me recruit players, I called Gustavo to tell him what had transpired, my dedication to the league, and to expect a call from that program. The host asked Gustavo to invite one member from each team to the show. All the teams were represented by one of their players in uniform with the exception of our team. For the Vikingos, Gustavo had one of the Lobos' players wear one of our new jerseys that I had just paid for.

＝+ +＝

Outside of friends and family, there were only a handful of fans at the games. I offered to print up a thousand tickets with the peso equivalent of roughly ten dollars on them. My idea was to divide them up amongst the players to give away for free to potential supporters in an effort to recruit fans. He shrugged me off like I was wasting his time. The playwright George Bernard Shaw said it best. People can't be helped. If a certain person needed to write a love letter and William Shakespeare climbed out of his tomb and told him how to write it, and then a stranger in the street advised him, he would listen to the stranger in the street.

I remember Oscar from the Gladiators telling me a story from his flag football days. One of the teams had recruited a guy in his mid forties working at the American embassy. Before becoming a diplomat, he had played cornerback for the Washington Redskins. In the huddle, he made a suggestion to the quarterback. The QB showed his appreciation with this reassurance: "You don't have to worry about that because I'm the coach." No surprise, the diplomat impeached himself from the team after that game. Some people can't be helped, and I'm a slow learner.

At the draft, I was called up onto the stage to make the first pick. There were two television personalities waiting for me there, a man in his forties and a voluptuous ex-model (bony don't cut it the Latin world) in her late twenties. Without encouragement on my part, she had been flirty with me earlier. Maybe my girlfriend had given her the evil eye, or vice versa. Not my first time being used as a pawn in this kind of match. They asked a few questions, with the final one from the guy being, "Aren't you afraid of all those young guys who want to hurt you?"

"You mean my feelings?"

"No, they told me they want to smash you into the turf?"

I just smiled at him and then looked over to the model and said, "I'm sorry, what is your name again?"

"Diana."

"Diana, I hope I'm not speaking out of turn, but I have to say you look incredibly lovely in that dress. Yet as great as you wear it, you should feel lucky that all those wannabe ladies from the other teams out there with their ties on were not allowed to wear their dresses to this event, because all of them are even more feminine and stunning than you in their dresses."

The players laughed. She smiled along, but underneath that grin, I could see she was not going to let her all powerful feminine aura be reduced to a mere prop for a joke in front of so many men. To put me in the weak-kneed place she was accustomed to men occupying in her presence, Diana put her arm over my shoulder and pulled me toward her. She began whispering something in my ear that I couldn't understand. I turned toward the players blushing, spinning my eyes in a cartoonish manner over exaggerating the feeling of being love struck. I stumbled into the microphone with a thud and replied, "I'm flattered, but I don't think the league will let you be my center."

The fuse had a three-second delay. If one earns the right to laugh by making other people laugh, that crack had me paid up for a year in advance! They were pounding the tables. Obviously, she got none of the joke until her compatriot explained it to her later on. Soon after, I feared that wisecrack might have crossed a boundary of respect. (Honestly, I considered that before, also, but if you never go for it on 4th down, you don't belong in the game.) When the event was finished and my girlfriend was in the bathroom, I went over to schmooze my way out of any possible offense. She gave me the perfunctory Argentine kiss, and then she handed me her card on which she had written "Call me." I guess she liked a challenge, too. Don't you just freakin' hate having a girlfriend at times like that?

With the first pick in the draft, we chose Sergio. He was a doctor soon to be moonlighting as a linebacker and tight end. He had played in the flag league, and was tough, strong, and a brutal blocker. We figured him for a good locker room leader. I would describe him as an All American, except for the fact that he wasn't American. Well, not American as North Americans think of Americans anyways.

Next round, I pushed Raul onto the stage to make the selection. We chose another guy from the flag football league named Julio. During camp, Julio was always mad about something or at someone. He hit pretty well and played above his size and with an abundance of emotion. Julio was the most competitive player at the camp. I hoped his distaste for people on the other side of the line would hold up through the season.

In the third round, we had a tough choice: a cerebral thirty something speedy cornerback, or an Argentine nineteen-year-old who had lived half his life in Connecticut. The kid loved football, stood 6'2", and had a super personality. He had met fellow ex-Connecticut resident Greg and wanted to play for us. The problem was that every time I saw him I had the urge to stuff a double cheeseburger into his mouth. He moved forward on two long toothpicks. There was no way I could imagine him lasting even half a game with all the ex-rugby players roaming the field looking for people to hurt. I guess I Pedro-principled between the second and third rounds. I chose the speedy cornerback, who proceeded to eschew the benefits of a vegetarian diet and lost weight every week as the kid gained weight and became a star at various positions for the Toros. The brainy cornerback, more than anyone I had met, helped explain the cultural differences between Argentina and the USA. The guy was so intelligent and well-spoken I almost hated to see him making tackles.

⊨⊣ ⊢⊨

Half my rap with the players was a poverty-stricken man's version of Don Rickles. Oddly enough, I was still a popular figure in the league. I regularly got mentioned on the Latin American broadcast of Monday night football. After exiting stage left from the event, I tried to understand how mostly fate had me living out this fantasy at my age in a strange and faraway land. I could barely rule out that I was the illegitimate son of Walter Mitty and George Plimpton.

That week we had a dinner at my house and handed out the uniforms. After the picture-taking of that pseudo ceremonious event, most started to pound beers. Greg was the clear leader in the quantity department. He challenged Rodrigo, soon to be re-named Arnold, to a chugging contest.

Rodrigo asked, "Are we betting?"

Greg offered, "If you lose, you have to come to practice for a month with a T-shirt saying "The Big G is my king." If I lose, which I won't, I have to run around the block naked."

Greg's rejoinder to the contract quickly spread to everyone in the room. If he was aware beforehand of Rodrigo's three-year apprenticeship in the land of the giant beer steins, it certainly did not enter into his inebriated mind then. I surely was not going to point out that detail to him. With everyone watching, I dropped my hand to signal the start. Rodrigo slammed his empty glass down, while Greg was barely crossing the 50 yard line.

I would like to think not one person in that room believed Greg would live up to his word—that is until he started pulling his clothes off in my hallway. I screamed, "What the F are you doing, you wacked-out drunk? I gotta live here. Let's get at least two blocks from the house before we see if you have the balls to live up to your word."

Even at that distance, I started getting colder feet than Greg's pecker was threatening to be. I asked our fireman center about potential repercussions. He laughed and told me he could likely smooth out any trouble that might come our way. Greg dropped his trousers, as I was kicking myself for dropping my homeowners insurance. The potential liability for supplying him the beer seemed as real as his naked ass. After he came back from his jog, as someone was speedily handing him his clothes, Greg said, "Hold on to them, I need to cool down first. Let's go somewhere and grab a beer." He started walking off buck-ass naked. There wasn't one guy who wasn't doubled over and gasping for breath far more so than Greg. Without any of the team ever having stepped on the football field with him, Greg became the fearless leader of the Vikingos.

Greg couldn't make the first practice of the Vikingos. At that practice, Stewart the "coach" showed up and decided the bouncer guy (who had never played a down of football in his life) would be the center and yell signals to call out the defense as he saw it. I thought, *What college team was Stewart on again, "My-imbecile of Ohio"? Okay, bouncer calls out the defense, and I am the captain of the H.M.S. Pinafore.*

After an hour of going over a few blocking techniques and his heroics in college, away from the other players, I relayed to coach the hell these guys had been through in camp. I asked him if we could play a game of touch football so that they could actually see how fun the game was. As I was playing defense alongside

Homer-the-Canuk, waiting for the offensive play, he feigned a yawn and then slowly enunciated, "Booor-inngg."

The guy with the ball from the offensive team ran by within a few feet of Homer, and he didn't make a move to chase him. I was perplexed, as I had never been bored even playing a game of two-on-two touch football. I felt like going off on the kid, *Hey stupido, all you've done is bitch about how bored you've been here in this town and now you are finally on a football field and you're still crying? Do you realize the effort involved just to get to this point? What did you expect? We would pad up the first night so that you could body-slam guys that have never played a minute of football in their lives? If you don't like it here, go back to your hostel and watch Colombian soap operas, you ungrateful dumb ass hillbilly, F you!*

Instead, I instituted "The Jordan Rules" and began coddling the head case. I calmly described the situation to him and called a time-out so that he could show everybody the different options you have as a runner on a pitch out. He explained them and demonstrated them better than I could have. I realized that this kid was going to require a lot of attention. I also figured even off the field, I would have to keep my mouth guard in just to keep me from biting through my lip. To understand why I instantly morphed into a patient father figure, you would have had to seen Homer the two or three times that he did hustle.

══╬ ╬══

Greg called me the following day to inform me that he'd had a change of heart and now wanted to be the coach. I told him that I had committed the job to Stewart and that I would have to go back on my word to him. He began selling himself for the job, including his having played in Holland, thus understanding how to teach at this level. I agreed with everything he had said. I remembered his analysis of the game we watched at Casa Bar. As much as I thought

I knew about the game from all the years of watching, his understanding was deeper, more instinctive, yet he made his opinions easy to understand. Besides being a good communicator, he had a player's perspective; I knew he should be the coach. In my short time around Stewart, I knew he should not be. I had also watched an NFL game with him, and his takes on the plays were as deep as that of the tackling dummy that he surely was in college.

I sucked it up and met Stewart for lunch. I used the legitimate excuse of his being away on business so much and that he had kids at home. I told him how I believed Greg needed this more than he did, as Greg lacked all the things that Stewart had in his life. Not perfect, but I was still learning how to kiss ass on the job. Stewart was slightly ticked, yet underneath appeared relieved at the same time. Relief only starts to describe how I felt that Greg was now the head coach. I used myself as the barometer. I was sure I could be a better head coach than Stewart and equally certain that I would not be better than Greg.

At his first practice, Greg yelled at a few players. That's perfectly acceptable for a football coach in our culture but not something done often in Argentine culture. Camp was one thing, but they believed they had put that nonsense in the rear view mirror. They took it without saying a word, but I could tell a few were irritated. Greg finally got around to screaming at me, and I replied feigning incredulousness, "Hey you can't yell at me, I'm the star." It got a big laugh. I wasn't trying to undermine his authority, but thought it best to show them not to take it personally or too seriously and that's just his way. Nobody was getting paid; in fact, they were paying dues to the league for the right to play. Greg always came with a plan. He left the responsibility of fitness to individuals on their own time. At our two weeknight practices, he concentrated on teaching fundamentals and his simple-to-understand plays. He taught with an enthusiasm that proved contagious and began to justify my maneuvering him into the position.

A SHARED EPIPHANY

At the second practice, I lofted a deep fly to Raul on the right sideline. I threw the ball over his right shoulder, and it sailed out of bounds. Raul and I talked the play over and then walked over to Greg for his opinion. I asked Greg to which shoulder the ball should be thrown on that pattern along the right sideline. "Throw it over the left shoulder, that way there's room to adjust for it. If you miss to the right, the ball is likely out of bounds. If you miss to the inside, he has room to go get it, and has a good shot at running for more yards. Even if you complete it over his right shoulder, his momentum is likely to carry him out of bounds."

That was a eureka moment for Raul and me. Call it a shared epiphany. We did not say a word; we just looked at each other with huge acknowledging smiles, knowing right then and there all of last year's types of tribulations were over. We were now learning from a superior.

If nothing else, Stewart was proving to be an excellent blocker and had a good suggestion now and then. The Dane was a stalwart, and Greg had the Gladiators castoffs, Martino and Ivan, playing better than I could have ever imagined. Between the above, the lack of Gladiators owner Manuel's mind games, and working out of the shotgun in obvious passing situations, I felt reborn.

Before our first scrimmage against the Toros, I walked over to five Gladiators players who were there to watch and began kidding with my old teammates. At first they were a little distant, uncomfortable, and then one joked, "Hey, you're the enemy."

I smiled and gave them the finger; then they all pounced on me. As I was at the bottom of the pile, it was if I had a pack of overtly friendly puppies all over me. That gesture of unbridled affection brought me back to a time in day camp at eight years old when a bunch of the other campers had sung about me ("For he's a jolly good fellow, which nobody can deny"). As we walked in separate directions I whispered, "Thanks for blinding me." I pretended to have gotten dirt in my eyes so that they wouldn't notice the real reason I wiped at them. As I walked away, I felt nothing like what had been sung about me now forty-four years back.

The Toros had a talented and cocky twenty-two-year-old American running back who also played well in various positions on defense. The QB had an adequate arm but excelled as a runner and was one of the best all-around athletes in the league. What the team lacked in football IQ, they made up for in team speed, especially at the corners. No score was kept, but they probably got the better of us—definitely of me. They were waiting on two of my deep throws and picked them off. Greg's strategy going in was to not show them too much of our playbook. Our rookies looked like rookies but still appeared thrilled to be out there in the heat of battle. I completed the last three passes I threw, which left me with a good deal of confidence going forward.

Homer brought his girlfriend to the following practice, and whenever he was on the sidelines, he tuned football out and his girlfriend's mouth in. Rather than throw cold water on them or yank them apart by their tails, Greg waited until they detached, pulled Homer aside, and chewed him out. "You're disrespecting me and the team. We're here to practice."

"But I'm bored."

"Then go home!"

I stopped Homer and his girlfriend as they were leaving and told him, "You were wrong. You owe Greg an apology."

"But I'm bored."

"What do you think it would be like if everyone made out with their girlfriends at practice? I understand your game is more advanced, but you have to be patient; they're new at this."

He gave Greg a whiny, half-assed apology, and we continued on with Greg still fuming. Minutes later, I tried to lighten Greg's mood with the following in a southern accent, "That boy just ain't right, just ain't right in the hay-id."

━┿ ┿━

The second and final scrimmage was against the Lobos. Manuel from the Gladiators was one of the refs; after he and Gustavo got a look at Homer up close and personal, I knew I was in their crosshairs. Looking at it from their perspective, I couldn't blame them. Against all their hopes and plans, I had the nerve to try to build a winning team.

On the first play, the offensive line missed most of their blocks, and Homer was gang-tackled behind the line of scrimmage, which prompted him to start yelling at our lineman. Going back to the huddle I asked Homer, "Do you think your time would be more productive at practice if instead of making out with your girlfriend, you worked with the O line on blocking technique?"

He nods, yes.

"Okay, then concentrate on doing the best you can do with what you have until then."

To get him in gear, Greg called a few runs for Homer behind the big Dane. Farm boy began to go through their line as if they were afraid of him. Greg caught the two passes I threw to him, but besides those, he kept himself out of the offensive scheme for both scrimmages. We scored almost at will. Raul was the thrilled recipient of most of the pass plays. On one pass play, Stewart was being covered by their smallest guy. I happened to know the guy and like him; hard not to, he always wore a smile and was quick with the wisecracks. After he knocked the ball from Stewart's hands causing an incomplete pass, Stewart started a fight with the little wolf. I was watching from the ground where their line had planted me. As I was getting up, Gustavo's buddy Esquiel was dropping a few stomps on Stewart. I didn't see how he got him down, but from what I had observed in practice, it wasn't a difficult task. Nothing I would describe as mayhem . . . more like measured and justifiable payback. By the time I jogged halfway over, the deed was done.

On the Lobos offensive, side when in the shotgun and their center snapped it poorly resulting in a loose ball, none of their team bothered to chase it down. They didn't score a point. Our team left the field pleased, but I'm not sure we built much confidence out of it, because the opposition had played with so little effort. I missed my first two passes and then hit six straight. My confidence was increasing as a result of that and the line play. In the locker room, Stewart balled out the whole team for not coming to his aid in a fight. I felt like having a private talk with him to let him know how wrong I thought he was, but I feared he would quit, as shortly before I had demoted him. At the time, I thought the cleat marks etched into his body would suffice to make the point better than I could have. Gustavo's maniacal buddy Esquiel started a fight every other week, and there were never consequences for him. If any of our players had engaged them, they would likely have been looking at a three- or four-game suspension. Yeah, it was that blatant. And I believe they dug blatant, because blatant sends a message of power. Stewart didn't get docked any games. I guess the on-field retribution that Gustavo's buddy had administered satisfied his sense of justice.

TOROS I: TAKING THE TOROS BY THE HORNS

Our first game was against the Toros who had just bested us in the scrimmage two weeks earlier. Club Peron had only splotches of grass here and there, which made the field similar to playing on cement. If wet, it was a slip-and-slide mud bath. It rained hard two nights prior to our contest. The following day dried only half the field, making it unpredictably treacherous the day of our game.

In the locker room before taking the field, everybody was pretty subdued. It was our first time playing in front of the other teams and the few fans. First time to remind the other players to take a leak, first time making sure my center had enough ball towels. The first time everything. The bouncer tough guy came over to me for reassurance. I was surprised to see him, of all people, nervous. I was standing on a bench getting my ankle taped as he was hovering below. I felt self-conscious when I gave him a pep talk, as if I were standing so far above him to play God. As many fights as this guy must have fought, there he was clinging to me like a puppy. I guessed with the gladiator-like armor on, he knew he was headed to an arena of battle in which he had never been tested. Fighters know fear better than most. The process of overcoming it and the accompanying sense of accomplishment . . . that's a hook for them. To slay your own dragons to control one's own spirit, that's part of sports, especially the combat variety. More than any other feeling, I was as alert and alive as I had ever been. I was taking in the room, its dialogue, and its movements. Greg was edgy about his socks not fitting right, groups of twos and threes chatting about what to expect, what do in this or that situation.

We had fifteen players on our squad. Nobody had us as the favorite, and I really had no idea how it would wind up. I stood on the sidelines watching Greg's defense hold them to a three and out. I took the field at our own 30. Homer opens with a 5-yard run. Next I hit Greg on a seven and out. We we're slightly past midfield, in the muddiest part of the pitch. Homer runs it to their 40. Greg calls a bomb to himself in the left side of the end zone. The muddy ball is snapped to me in the shotgun; I fiddle with it trying to get the laces, if not any grip. No laces, no real grip, my internal clock forces me to let it go. It feels more like a shot put than a pass. I regret letting it go the second it leaves my hand—and more so as it waddles down the field. Greg stabs it out of the air surrounded by two defensive backs; it falls off his hand, and hits their cornerback in the chest, and bounces back into Greg's hands, 6 points. I feel lucky that it landed anywhere near him. Our 2-point run attempt gets stuffed, leaving it at 6-0 us.

Their running quarterback is quickly getting frustrated with his lack of footing and the variety of blitzes Greg is calling on almost every play. We pick him off at our 40. I hand it to Homer, who runs it to their 37. Greg lines up on the right, calls for another bomb to him in the right side of the end zone. About 15 yards into his route, he dips his inside shoulder, dropping his head even more so as a fake, before veering to the right to fly downfield. Their line blocks my view, so I can't see him coming out of his break as he takes off. I wait two seconds, relying strictly on timing; I hit him in stride at around the 5. I witnessed nothing of the touchdown, I only saw my teammates looking downfield and raising their hands. I get a couple of pats on the helmet, and I give a couple of pats on the helmet. I had figured out last season that I had enough energy to play, but I didn't have enough to run across the field to celebrate every little success and play football, also.

Julio and Sergio are all over the field making defensive plays. The beer-chugger-extraordinaire Arnold is on almost every special team's tackle. The Toros can do nothing offensively. I pass, to a triple-covered Raul in the right corner for 6 more. They are out of sorts and screaming at one another. I take no pleasure in watching them come apart. I like everybody on that team; none take cheap shots. I feel they are paying too much reverence to my age rather than slamming and burying me when they get their chances. I think it best to wait until now to share that sentiment with them.

As a rule, we opted for the 2-point conversion. Although in soccer-mad Argentina, half the Argentines on the team could kick a 30-yard field goal. As hard as we tried, we couldn't make a consistent long snapper out of anyone. Once with a 6-point lead, we went for it on 4th and 7 from our own 40. Different variables than a pro or college game; our snapper had muffed over half of them in the practices leading up to that contest.

Near the end of the game, they throw a midrange pass to their springy receiver. Greg cuts in front of him and jumps to block the ball but doesn't get high enough. Six points the other way. As Greg has been a pretty serious taskmaster, and we were still up 40 to 6, I think everybody is taking that play with a sigh of relief. We all now feel less pressure to be perfect. Good thing, because I missed one of my nine passes. The final score is 40-7 us.

As I was sitting on my folding chair watching the second game, a couple of the Toros, including the American kid, came over to me in utter frustration to settle arguments amongst themselves. I told them, "The most important thing for you guys is not to focus on the score. When you get behind you have to press, try risky plays, and the more those risks don't pay off, the more you are forced to take even bigger risks. That's why the score means less than you think. The key for you guys is to stick together, analyze the DVD, and correct mistakes. Do you think, because the final score was 40-7, that I believe we are over five times better than you? One game proves little. If you had gotten the first lucky touchdown that we did, the momentum easily could have swung the other way. Same goes for our team; we can't overestimate the significance of the final score."

One of the unforeseen benefits of playing for and running the team was that I was gaining firsthand validation of nearly half a century's worth of commentary I'd heard from NFL broadcasters, coaches, players, and owners. For the prior forty-five years, it had been just that: commentary. Now, that verbiage was taking on a deeper significance and coming to life in handy ways. I believed I instinctively knew what to do with the ball in almost every situation. I knew what to remind the other players of in the huddle. My helmet wasn't wired for sound; yet it was as if Chris Collingsworth and Phil Simms were in it giving me their advice. If I'd had the ability, I would have set up a verbal alarm clock to wake to the voice of an early Jets television analyst Al Derogodis. I loved Nina Simone and Harry Belafonte's voices, but I preferred Curt Gowdy's, for his signaled the start of my favorite day: football Sunday.

STALLIONS I: ADMITTEDLY, I WANTED MY WARM BLANKIE

The field is muddier than the week before. It's cold and wet, and the game is starting at dusk with poor lighting. They are coached and quarterbacked by the coach of last year's National team, he of helmet-gate fame. His treatment of me at the National team tryouts still stings. Standing in the way of my revenge is a 300-pound Peruvian weightlifting champion, along with the rest of their defensive linemen, who are all above 6'2" and also take up a lot of space in the other direction. They have five guys who played in Peru's highest-caliber league.

We trade two futile possessions each, and we now have it at our 30. I get sacked on 1st down for a 6-yard loss. On 2nd down, Homer runs into a wall and is stopped for no gain. It seems like a stalemate; we're both stuck in the mud in every sense of the word. On 3rd down, the ball is snapped to me in the shotgun; I see their line busting through right and left, so I tuck it and run up the middle. I twist out of a tackle well short of the original line of scrimmage; a vicious helmet-to-helmet shot courtesy of the guy whose ass I booted in the camp's gauntlet rocks me. I'm stopped in my tracks; the noise reverberates all over the field. Their sideline lets out a deep "*Ewwww!*" Maybe their guys on the field were too busy admiring the hit, also, because no one finishes the job; I continue running through traffic in what I hope is the right direction. I'm grabbed and then fall forward for the 1st down.

As I walk back to the huddle, I return a mocking "*Ewwww*" to their bench. I've been down this same road with Peruvians. Standing in shotgun before I start my count, while looking at the defense, I sing out, "Besame mucho." Three seconds after the snap, while looking downfield for a receiver, my legs get chopped out from under me; I stay down momentarily with a twisted knee. I already knew that I can't sing; I guess I needed that painful hit to teach me not to sing! Greg moves to QB and runs the ball out of the shotgun when not handing it to Homer. We march the rest of the way down the field to score 6. Greg's toss to Raul for the 2 points is incomplete. We flub the kickoff, and they now have it at our 35.

They move a few yards closer on a run and then throw for a touchdown. On the conversion, their trick play opens a receiver in the end zone for 2, making it 8-6 them. I come back only to spell Greg when he needs a breather. It makes sense. He's more mobile, even more so with my knee tightening. It's too dark to see the receivers downfield; we have to run. We trade touchdowns, except this time we make our 2 and they don't. Regulation time ends in a 14-14 tie.

Their QB, and halfback along with Greg, me, and the refs meet at midfield. One of the refs asks, "Would you like to call it a tie or play an overtime period?"

It's cold and I'm soaking wet. While I begin to contemplate my warm blankie waiting for me at home, Greg snaps at the refs, "F ties—we play to win." I have no idea what the Stallions wanted to do, but after Greg's proclamation, they had to agree to play or look like cowards.

We kick to them, and they march it down for a field goal. As we have no field goal team, we need 6 or it's a loss. As best I could see in the near dark from our sidelines, Greg and Homer take turns ramming it down their throats for the win. I wish I could have done more to help, but I was impressed with and gained confidence in our entire team, especially Greg's killer instinct.

Normally the enemy combatants change in separate lockers, but as one was under repair, we share. I walk over to their halfback and compliment him on his game. Then I yell across the room to the guy who rattled my cage, "Hey *umbros de piedra* (shoulders of stone, inspired by boxer Roberto Durán's famed nickname manos de piedra, or hands of stone)—nice hit!"

He walks over to me and asks me, "How's your knee?"

"It's nothing serious, thanks. How's your head? I think it ran into set concrete."

Then Greg yells from across the room to *umbros de piedra*, in reference to me, "You made him look like a dashboard bobblehead doll going over railroad tracks."

Without looking at Greg, yet loud enough for him to hear, I ask the Peruvian if he wants him for a fifth-round draft choice next year. We all laugh and become fast friends after that. I feel especially good about this new friendship, because I never felt especially good about my stunt with him in the rookie camp.

I walk over to their quarterback and tell him, "There was no loser tonight; you played great." It was true; he helped his team more than I helped mine. He said nothing in return. I don't hold it against him; just write it off to him being a tough competitor.

MY HOME AWAY FROM HOME

My physical therapist is also the trainer for the Pumas, the national rugby team. Maybe he gets bored yanking on limbs, or possibly he wants to create more work for himself, because he was constantly pitting me against the rugby players. One day, the trainer overheard me answering a question from a rugby player as to why we wear pads. From that day forward, he prompted any rugby player within sight: "Pssst, ask the gringo why rugby players don't wear helmets and pads like American football players."

After the player obliged him, I would respond, "Because they don't hit hard enough to need them." If the player wasn't too big, I customized it to, "Because *you* don't hit hard enough to need them."

The Monday after the Stallions game, he leads me to a small treatment room and opens the door. Spread out on a medical table—at least what parts of him fit on it—is a guy who even without all the wires attached to him could be mistaken for Frankenstein. Being routinely shocked to stimulate his muscles has no effect on the monster's sleep. Accounting for the size of him, one might have to consider that the machine didn't have enough volts to have an impact.

The therapist calls out his name loudly a few times before the guy moves his headphones off his cauliflower ears and asks, "What's up?"

The trainer tells him to "ask the gringo why rugby players don't wear helmets and pads like American Football players."

After the giant obliges him, I follow the script above. As you're learning, yeah, I'm *stupido* like that, especially when prompted. He begins to snarl and starts to rise up. My only question is whether he's going to confront me verbally or just pounce. The floors and walls are not padded like a jujitsu gym, and this agitated lummox is all about tackling people. Rather than look for a breaker switch on the wall to pull down in the hopes of decommissioning the monster, I go with a very friendly, "Just kidding, just kidding, amigo." I turn and leave as quickly as my stiff knee will let me. I look at the therapist and say, "What's wrong with that guy? He can't take a joke?"

"He's the team's enforcer."

We both laugh, but mine is quieter as I fear instigating the goon. At a safe distance, I turn to the therapist and demand in a deep voice, "F-e-e-d . . . m-e . . . c-o-o-k-i-e."

EVERYBODY COMES WITH DISCLAIMERS

For Friday night's light practice before our next game with the Lobos, I rent a mini soccer field. Stewart encourages me to do that often, because the lighting is so much better than the park in which we normally practice. He tells me he'll pitch in on the cost; I'm still waiting for peso one. There are six small fields jammed in to fit the space in an urban area. Me, Greg, Homer, and a few others get there early and toss the ball around to loosen up. On another field a few yards below us and perpendicular to ours, there's some sort of league soccer game going on. Around thirty fans overflow their small viewing area. One team's uniforms match the orange ball. It looks like a serious to-do.

In the middle of the game, their ball sails over the goal and rolls right to Homer. He picks it up, and rather than toss it the 15 or so yards back to them, he attempts to drop kick it in their direction. For a reason that would likely short-circuit Sigmund Freud's brain if he risked trying to understand why, Homer kicks it with all of his might. It goes off the side of his foot and lands on the roof of a neighboring building. There is a silent pause for all to take in and absorb the moronic action. Soon, the beating of war drums can be heard in the near distance. Putting on an expression that most resembles a white flag, and with my hands raised as if to signal not to shoot, I jog over to their field and tell the guy who walks to meet me, "I'm sorry, I'll be happy to pay for it." Tilting my head back in the direction of Homer, forcing my eyes up and to the right, as if I am trying to look behind my head, I then say, "Forrest Gump." A few chuckle, and the guy tells me not to worry, they have plenty more and know how to get that one later. I'm not sure if it was my skill in humoring him that saved our necks or the possibility that every team has at least one Gump.

I remember nothing else of that practice other than chatting with Homer and four or five teammates afterward in the parking lot. It's a small space, with the cars packed in tight. We have a duffel bag with our equipment sitting in the middle of the driveway. A car pulling in appears not to see the bag. Homer has a football in one hand and his first beer in the other. To signal the driver to stop, Homer's version of resourceful communication has him head butting the driver's side window twice. (No, he did not have a helmet on.) The guy jumps out ready to fight. I walk over only as fast as I feel I can without appearing threatening and tell the guy, "Sorry, he's a kid and has had more beers than he can handle." The guy grumbles and gets back in his car. I look over at Homer and give him the most pronounced *What the F?* look I have ever given in my long history of giving *What the F?* looks. In response to my expression, Homer points to the bag on the ground with his head, and then looks back at me slightly perturbed, as if I were falsely accusing him. In his mind, obviously it was the guy in the car who was at fault and the stupid one.

⇒+ +⇐

As I had a strong feeling of responsibility for my teammates, before that first game with the Toros I had ordered five new helmets and shoulder pads from a website in the United States. My rationale was that those five sets would keep my players from the worst of the worst that the league supplied. As I had learned at customs the year before, it is cost prohibitive to ship to Argentina. I flew twelve hours in each direction and picked them up. As I proudly placed them on the sidelines at practice, it looked like a fumble drill as the players fought over them. It became all too clear: to stave off a mutiny, I would need at least two more helmets. I figured Stewart earned as much or more than I did. Still, rather than approach him about buying his own equipment, I asked, "Hey, Stewart, next week when you're in the States, if I have two helmets shipped to your hotel, can you bring them down?"

"No."

"Well, then just one?"

"No, I can't."

He didn't offer a reason. I was so taken aback by his tone that I didn't ask him for one. He was traveling for half the practices; surely he couldn't still be upset about Greg replacing him as the coach.

Weeks later, in a taxi on the way to our first game against the Lobos, I get a call from Stewart: "If I don't get the new medium helmet, I am not coming to the game."

I should be subjected to one of the ten plagues of Egypt for not reminding him about his rejection of my request to bring a helmet down before the Toros game. Then I should be punished with the other nine plagues for not telling him not to come and to go F himself. At the field, I get the same ultimatum from Homer for the new extra-large helmet. I couldn't understand what he was so worried about when, despite the physical size of the helmet's soon-to-be contents, he had so little to risk.

⊫ ⊨

Understandably, not too many people on our team wanted to hang out with Homer and his girlfriend. On Friday nights, they liked to escape their hostel and come over for dinner and a movie in my TV room. For my bonus, they would also spend the night. I was within their budget, and they looked up to me, as I was the only one who had the patience and enough motivation to deal with them. At least on Friday nights before games, keeping him away from the public at large had an upside.

I told Homer on three occasions that walking around my house in his tighty-whities was making my girlfriend uncomfortable. He never grasped the concept. I only hoped he didn't think her hair appeared soft because I feared I had Lenny from *Of Mice and Men*, semi-streaking through my house. Homer and his girlfriend were only scheduled to be in Buenos Aires enough time for him to play in six of the scheduled ten games. As proof of the amount of self- and girlfriend-sacrifice involved in trying to win football games, I was encouraging them to stay for the full season. In truth, at a certain point, even without his huge benefit to our team, I felt attached and committed enough to try to help him get by.

Deep down, I liked Homer, principally, because he liked me. There was no sneakiness or guile to him. I believed that would be the case even if he had the mental capacity for those evils. He was just a very immature nineteen. Strictly going on looks, he could pass for twenty-three, which only exaggerated that immaturity. As many teenagers, and people of every age who never properly address and work on their issues, he had some personality defects. His poor communication skills led him to frustrate easily and demonstratively. Although he was more than a handful, I liked him more as I began to understand him better. I felt closer to him than anyone else on the team. Being needed will do that to you.

⇌╫⇌

On a certain level, I liked Gustavo of growing league control fame also. To begin to figure him out, I had to realize he was raised in another culture that was *mucho* different from what I was accustomed to. I often needed to remind myself that I was playing in his league and living in his country. Naturally, many of the things I took for granted as being the correct way, he saw differently. While he wasn't the gregarious type, I found his personality pleasing. He commanded respect, yet there wasn't a drop of cockiness or arrogance to him. . . . Yeah, I'm aware of some of my flaws. . . . He was plenty smart in certain areas. As a politician, he was more than capable; he made sure he had friends with big ears on every team. I assumed the denouncements of him that I used to motivate our team, before games against squads on which he had good friends, got back to him. I took those risks with him because the more like-minded president was able to hold him in check via a stalemate with the league's votes. As many of our players had amigos on the other teams, I created an enemies list from all the squads, with colorful rationale included to help provoke our players into the aggression needed to succeed on the field. Not sure how much it helped them, but it worked for me.

I really did appreciate the work Gustavo had done to help create my personal Argentine fantasy camp, which made me all the more frustrated that he would not let me help him. Part of his unwillingness to let me help him, could have been my fault. On one occasion in my first year, he did ask for my help. Gustavo called to tell me a high school coach from the United States was coming to discuss bringing a high school all-star team from his state to play our national team. Five of us went to an all-you-can-eat steak buffet. If you got through the preface of this book, you know the cow is cut up differently here, so as the coach was getting up to make his choices on the various cuts that I was still a rookie about, I asked Gustavo to go help him with his selections. All I needed to add was, *Hey, Gustavo, could you go help instead of me? I'm still figuring out what's what with the different cuts.* I realized my faux pas as they were walking away. In spite of having twenty years on him, who in the hell was I to tell him to do anything, especially in front of his peers? After the meal, I put my arm around him and humbly apologized, telling him that I was out of line and something to the effect of *I would have gone with the coach had I been able to understand how the cow ate the cabbage in terms of getting itself butchered.* Side note: When in the states, I don't upset myself by ordering meat.

I believed he denigrated the legitimacy of the league by playing favorites to the extreme. Maybe this is what he had to do in his world to stay in power. I never felt like he got the big picture or envisioned the potential of the league that I imagined. Brazil started drawing thirty thousand people four years after they kicked their first ball that wasn't round. Obviously Gustavo knew more about how Argentina works than I did. Possibly if he were to try to maximize the league's potential, bigger sharks with the law on their side would pull it away from him. Clearly you're not reading a book taking in place in Kansas! Many small businesses around the world want to stay small for various legitimate reasons; I hope he had his. Maybe he felt he would get obliterated him if he tried to command anyone more advanced than the twenty-something's he successfully manipulated. We would yap back and forth on friendly terms about league matters, with neither of us giving the other much of our real thoughts. Although I made little headway bantering with Gustavo, he was at least interesting. The real danger that I foresaw was that his buddy Esquiel was starting to make gains, intimidating Manuel-the-swing-vote away from his ally the president to their side.

⊷ ⊶

I kept up with my jujitsu training during the season, because lifting weights bored me. I looked upon this martial art as a type of yoga, albeit the involuntary kind. Bouncer man took private classes from a high-level black belt who had spent a good deal of time training in Brazil. He encouraged me to go practice with his instructor. I finally took him up on it after my instructor left for Uruguay. As I was the new guy on the mats and had not yet established my place in the pecking order, all his students went extra-hard during training matches. After one class, I had a slight pain or soreness in my throwing shoulder that would not go away. I wasn't particularly worried because I took extra time to stretch anyways.

LOBOS I: RABID D-LINE

G ustavo's cheap-shot artist-friend Esquiel's apparent main job was to try to intimidate players on the other teams. Before our game, as I am off stretching on my own, he approaches me with a scowl and starts growling threats. Esquiel is a stocky 6'3". I stayed in his face, with only a slight twist of my position to shield my below-the-belt T Formation, and laughingly asked, "Is it really true that you shave your ass and then your face in that order before every game?" He laughed and walked away. I would not go so far as to say I liked him, but I did get a kick out of him. Off the field he was an intelligent guy with a managerial job, but no matter his surroundings, you could still see flashes of that cheap-shot artistic temperament.

They receive the kickoff and run it back to midfield. All that good field position served to do for them was give Raul a little more exercise as he picked off the first pass and ran it all the way back for 6 points. Greg runs the conversion in from out of shotgun, taking us to an 8-0 lead.

On their next possession, it's 3rd and short; they sweep right with their little halfback carrying the ball. It's the same little person that Stewart had picked the fight with in the scrimmage. Homer is running full speed from his middle linebacker position and has him in his sights. He intentionally lands with all his weight on him. It looks as if he is bodysurfing him out of bounds. No 1st down, but the guy still jumps up with a smile on his face. They punt it back to us. On our next play, from scrimmage, as I'm dropping back with Esquiel bearing down on me primed to finally express his feelings on a physical level, I rush the pitch to Homer. It's a little long, he bobbles it and it hits the ground. They pick it up and run it the other way for a touchdown. For all the assets Homer has as a football player, good hands are not one of them. No excuses, as even this early in the season Greg had bailed me out on two pitches that should have been fumbles. It's now 8-6 in our favor.

Their quarterback is Gustavo's Chilean pal. He's fast, has a strong arm, and throws a tighter spiral than I do. The problem is he likes to throw moving backward and doesn't find it important to point his body at the target. It was as if he wanted to make each throw more challenging. I felt funny about approaching him directly, so on various occasions I told Gustavo, "Give me your Chilean friend for half an hour and then you'll see the best quarterback in the league." Either he had a bad memory or just didn't want my help for any reason, because I never got to work with his buddy. He would often miss his receivers by 15 or 20 yards, if in fact I was guessing correctly who his targets were as he whipped his passes haphazardly across his body.

They go 3 and out, and punt it back to us. I take turns handing it to Esteban, Greg, and finally Homer for another 6 points. I get sacked on the 2-point conversion, leaving it at 14-6 us.

Again they go three and out, and kick it back to us. The first play, That's-My-Boy runs it for 6 yards to the Lobos 40. Next, I get the ball in the shotgun formation. I see their defensive end on my left, bee-lining it for me. I wait until I feel he is committed to his path, and then I run up into the pocket like a javelin thrower, as much to avoid him as to get the power to heave it to Greg, who's behind the triple coverage in the end zone. Touchdown, I raise my arms up and let my guard down. Their end, Guillermo, plays chiropractor with my lower back. Standing above my center on the 2-point conversion, one of their linebackers screams, "See that ambulance over there, old man? You are leaving in it." I audible and run the 2-point conversion in.

As I lay on the ground in the end zone, I feigned the voice of an old man and wailed, "Help me, I've fallen and I can't get up." That rendition of the famous Life Alert commercial was lost on them. So when I did get up, I hiked my stretch pants up to my chest, leaned forward as far as I could, and, on unsteady knees, mimed holding myself up with a rickety cane. Not the touchdown dance I would have choreographed beforehand, but I felt the need to pander to my audience. We are up 22-6.

Their runback gets them good field position, and their little guy busts a long one for a TD. They convert the 2, bringing them to within 8. The score stays the same, until we march down the field to put it out of reach with another 6 points. We win 28-14.

AGUILAS I: LOYALTY, SHMOYALTY

The Aguilas have good team speed and that jumbo-size line-man I feared more than the giant Peruvian of the Stallions. This guy was much faster and had a larger appetite for quarter-backs. Their QB's limited knowledge of the game came under the tutelage of Sony PlayStation. He had the arm of a seventh-grader but was a speedy and crafty runner. His biggest flaw was he ran out of bounds as if they awarded points for it. The team had moved over from the flag-football league and tackled like they had never left it. They had a few weak links on defense, none more so than one of their outside linebackers who started only because he was also the coach.

We start on our 24, Homer goes up the middle for 7. Then I rifle it to Greg at the line of scrimmage, who takes it for a 1st down and a few more. Homer for 5, Homer for 10, Homer sweeps right, gets stymied at the line of scrimmage, and reverses field to run along the other sideline for 20. *Okay, Homer, torture me off the field,*

I can deal with it! Next play, under center, I fake a handoff up the middle, then float a perfect spiral to Greg in stride in the back of the end zone. We miss the 2, 6-0 us.

They get the ball back and can't make it move forward until they boot it back to us. Greg spells me on the majority of the next possession, as he and Homer take turns running it. Homer plows through the middle from 3 yards out for the score. Again we miss the 2, 12-0 us. They get the ball back and kick it back from about where they started. They are blitzing most plays, and there isn't much time for me to throw. We have a decent lead, so now it's my turn to hand it off to Greg, That's-My-Boy, and Homer, culminating in another 6. This time Greg runs the 2 in to make it 20-0 us.

On their next possession, they go 3 and out, and once again return it to us via a swinging foot. Greg orders up a little target practice for me on a called play to him. I roll out of the pocket and am hesitant to risk throwing it to him along the right sideline. We have a substantial lead and he's double covered. Greg yells, "Throw that F'n thing!" I let *that F'n thing* go and hit him for a 30-yard pickup at their 40. Our drive stalls on a few runs right there. One of those runs had me scrambling out of the pocket and running along the left sideline until their combination coach/linebacker falls in front of me and sticks his leg out, imitating a soccer tackle. I am ticked off because my knee was too heavily taped to try to jump over his offending appendage. We trade punts, and have the ball back on our own 5 yard line early in the fourth quarter. Their defense holds, and we flub the punt; they land on it for a safety. It's now 20-2 us.

We choose to punt it back to them. We're giving them the short passes because of the time left and the score. They march down and throw for a TD, and make their 2, making it 20-10 us.

I often think of the "prevent defense" as the "prevent winning defense." I understand that it is a math equation and the smart move most of the time, but I often look at it as a self-administered torture device for the leading team to gift a nearly beaten team momentum and a new life.

One of the shortcomings of our league was that it had no game clock other than the stopwatch in the referee's hand. I found it a great distraction to have to scream at the ref for how much time was left. One of our players had offered to make a game a clock and gift it to the league; they declined, go figure. I did, and this is what I came up with: Why take the power away from the referees, whom they employ, and put it in the hands of a clock that everyone can see? Circuit boards and light bulbs are not amenable to schmoozing. I know that techies are making great strides with artificial intelligence, but to simulate the real human thought process they will also have to design into their devices artificial chicanery.

We have the ball back on our 10. Greg is in at QB, because clearly we are in a running situation with the lead and the pocket watch winding down. The handoff exchange between him and Homer lands on the ground, and an Aguila falls on it in the end zone for another 6 plus the 2. So 20-18 us is our new reality.

I now scream for the time remaining every play; I get a response every other play. There are less than two minutes to go, and they have no time-outs. We try to kill the clock with three running plays up the middle, but that doesn't suffice. Go figure. You shouldn't need my help this time. We punt it back to them; they run it back to midfield. They throw a long pass up the middle, Greg picks it off, and the ref signals the game is over.

After the whistle blows, Greg gives his on-field post-game summation and advice in an admonishing tone for the first time. "When we have a big lead and are looking to run out the clock, you have to block for the run like you are losing. First downs give you the win."

In the team's consolidated immature football mind, they were ripe to be swayed by the locker-room mutterings of Raul and Stewart. "It was Greg's fault that they came back and almost beat us because he changed our normal MO of throwing it often. He played too conservative."

Greg, obviously lacking X-ray vision, was just playing the referee's stopwatch as best he could. On top of that, he had seen me pancaked enough times to know it was too risky to throw it under the circumstances.

In the locker room, Raul, who had been holding his frustration back about not getting enough passes so far this season, uses the mounting ill will he helped create to find the courage to ask Greg why he isn't getting more throws his way. Greg passed him the truth, "Because I am better than you."

When I reviewed the DVDs, it was only a 60 percent to 40 percent split in thrown-to times in favor of Greg.

That night I get a call from Greg, who had witnessed the poison of Raul and Stewart manifest itself amongst the players. "If they're not happy with me, I'll quit right now."

"You called a great game. You did what you had to do; I had no time to throw. They thought they had the game won and stopped blocking. You're dealing with a bunch of football ignoramuses, pay them no mind."

"I don't need that crap from those idiots."

"Greg, you've taken a new team, an undermanned team of mostly outcasts and neophytes. You have them undefeated through four games. The defense is playing great; the simple schemes are perfect for their simple selves. On the other side, I wouldn't call you the offensive coordinator, more like an offensive choreographer. That's what it feels like from my perspective. I expect every play to work. It's a nine-man dance, and you have it in sync. You keep doing what you've been doing; I'll straighten them out."

One by one, I explained to the players the merits of Greg's strategy.

"He didn't have to yell at us."

"Oh stop, that's just how he works. Do I break down in tears when he yells at me? You want me to buy you a candy bar?"

It surprised and disappointed me that half of the team swallowed the locker-room nonsense spewed by the emotionally undernourished Raul and Stewart. Worse was how easily the team's loyalty could be swayed.

I don't like on-field celebrations after wins; they make me feel like we're rubbing the victory in our opponents' faces. I went over to them but stayed to the outside of the scrum, patted a few backs and walked away. After what I saw in this locker room, it inhibited my celebrations even more so.

GLADIATORS I: BITTERSWEET

The thought of playing against a team filled with friends was unsettling. I tried to overcome that by thinking of our undefeated record. Still I didn't relish the thought of seeing them lose, especially coach Dario, as he took the losses so hard. The idea of our Vikingos taking its first loss was even less appealing. The Gladiators had dropped their first two games and were now on a two-game winning streak.

We meet at the 50 for the coin toss; Santiago, their defensive leader and another player for the them are wearing Mexican wrestling masks. The colorful pageantry has me and others cracking up. Once we take the field, I couldn't wait to get hit to snap me into the aggressive mode I was struggling to find. On the first play from scrimmage, Santiago blitzes from middle linebacker and obliges me as if he had been privy to my thoughts. If he had been, he must have lost something in the translation, as I didn't mean *that hard* or behind the line of scrimmage!

Stewart yells at me, "What was wrong with the blocking on that one? You should've got the pass off."

It irritates me, until I quickly understand that his behavior is that of a dog well accustomed to being kicked. "You're right, I should have."

After going backward 7 yards on the first down sack, we couldn't make up the extra distance, and we punt; it rolls to their 30.

My rookie replacement on the Gladiators throws a pick for daring to throw near Greg. First play on our new series, I target Greg, who bobbles it for a rare drop. I hit Stewart for a more predictable drop. I hand it to Homer, and he fumbles it over to them. They take advantage of the miscues a few plays later with a TD and a 2-point conversion to put them up 8-0.

Stewart drops another short pass. I have never shown anger or even frustration with drops. If the receiver apologizes: "Nothing to be sorry for, I miss more passes than you drop." I loathe players who yell at or criticize teammates on the field. It's almost always counterproductive. Rolling right, I hit Raul going the other way across the middle for a 1st down. Their defense holds on the next series, and we are forced to punt it back to them. They go 3 and out, and send on the punting team. Greg loads one side of the line, which confuses them, leading to a fumbled snap that Victor recovers at their 37.

I fire it to Greg at the sideline. They gang-tackle him 5 yards out of bounds and shove him into a picnic table on the other side of the fence opening. The cheap shot almost came back to bite them immediately, as Greg misses landing on their coach's four-year-old boy by inches. After that stunt, all mixed emotions are gone; I only think about beating them. Me, Greg, Homer, and That's-My-Boy take turns running it down their throats. That's-My-Boy blasts the final 10 yards up the middle for his first touchdown. He then, for reasons a soccer fan would better understand, starts running the other way down the field while trying to remove his jersey. Greg and I start screaming at him to come back. We get a delay of game penalty. Regardless of the extra 5 yards, Greg runs the 2 in for the tie.

They return the kickoff all the way into our end zone; luckily, it gets called back for a block below the waist. Thank God Manuel is playing, not refereeing. He is far more dangerous with a whistle in his mouth than with a helmet on his head. Their rookie QB has a strong arm and can throw an accurate deep ball but short-arms most of his other passes. His best attribute is as a runner; good cuts, better speed. He relies on his legs to take them on a march to our 30. This is becoming a little scary until we pick him again at our goal line. From there we dink-pass and run our way to our 25. On the next play, one of their linebackers jerks me to the ground by my face mask. I don't do anything but give him a friendly pat when I get up. I have no idea of the extent of the infraction until I watch the DVD a few days after.

That linebacker was a quiet and mild-mannered guy, until he got in the driver's seat of a car, where he instantly morphed into a hostile lunatic. Maybe he mistook my face mask for a steering wheel. Who knows? I just feel lucky that my previously jujitsu-herniated neck discs C6 and C7 are still in place.

The following play called is a hesitation screen to Sergio, our tight end lined up on the right. I get the snap in shotgun and instinctively roll right as they are blitzing everybody up the middle. Normally for this play to work, Sergio needs to wait and sell himself as a blocker first, which he is doing. On a blitz my well-being needs less hesitating and more waving of his arms to signal *Hey I'm open!* As Santiago is dropping a hand on my helmet, Sergio, unaware of my plight, is still looking downfield; I have little choice but to float it ahead of him and hope the route he finally starts runs him under it. He reaches in front of him and grabs it in stride near the right sideline.

I hear Greg scream, "Oh gawwwd, he caught it!"

After 20 yards, a linebacker who has the angle on Sergio catches up to him and throws his arms out to make the tackle. Sergio straight-arms him in the chest, and the would-be tackler stumbles to the ground. Some 25 yards later, the fastest corner in the league is gaining on Sergio at what appears to be twice his speed. Sergio's missile defense comes in the form of another stiff arm, and the skinny guy drops to his knees like he's been shot. Sergio lifts the ball over his head at the 5 and runs into the end zone that way. I'd rather premature ejaculate on the three first attempts at pleasing the love of my life than watch one premature celebration. The brilliance of his run counters my disgust with the early self-salutation. On the conversion, Greg busts two tackles and we get 2 points for his effort, pushing it to 16-8 us.

They can't complete any of their next three passes and boot it back to us. Greg calls the same hesitation screen to Sergio. Rolling right, again I lob it to him in stride for the completion. Santiago, who was sitting out this play, screams from the sideline, "Oh no, not again!" In spite of all the friendships, I get a sense of satisfactions hearing that cry of resignation. Hey, I can beat friends in Ping-Pong without getting all emotional, so what's the difference? This copy goes for fifteen. We run a few times, and Greg tells me to call whatever I like as he heads to the sideline for a break. I get greedy and call a deep post. Their speed guy who got pole-axed by Sergio picks it off and runs it back to their 40. That's my first interception of the year. They run a few times, and Victor stuffs them for no gain on 3rd down and they have to kick it back to us.

Greg and Homer do their ground-game thing, and we put it out of reach with another touchdown and 2-point conversion. The end tally is 24-8 us. After the final whistle, I run over to Coach Dario and give him a pat on the back. I tell him how lucky I feel to come away with the win. "The game was a lot closer than the score indicated." I yap with a few of my old friends on the Gladiators and then head to the showers. I am enjoying the victory more than I thought I could.

STALLIONS II: "OH, MY POOR LEG IS TIRED"

The Monday before the Saturday game, I came down with the flu. I didn't have the strength or courage to get out of bed as result of the chills. I had wanted at the Stallions bad, but lacked the energy to even get upset about not being in condition to play. Thursday I am feeling no better and resigned to the likelihood of not going to the game let alone suiting up to play. That same night, five of the players who were out at a sports bar near my apartment stopped in to see me. They came into the bedroom and gave me encouragement and told me they knew I would be better by Saturday. I missed both practices that week. Guilt hit as soon as they left. Friday I woke up feeling slightly better; Saturday I awoke almost forgetting how sick I felt all week.

I own a pair of sunglasses that have an MP3 player built into them. I mainly use them for cycling, but as my warm-up routine is getting longer by the week, I bring them to the game to alleviate the boredom. As I walk over to chat with a few of the Stallions who also show up way before game time, I'm forced to play show-and-tell.

As a player I know as CIA tries them on and fiddles with the buttons, he says, "Will you give them to me if we beat you?"

I reply, "I'll give them to you now if you promise not to hit me." As violent as that team was, I always found them entertaining and a great bunch of guys. We joke back and forth before I beg out with, "I got to get some extra stretching in because I have a good idea what you have planned for me."

It was difficult to get our team to come early enough so that we could have a proper warm-up together. Part of the problem was that our leader, Greg, was an insomniac who showed up at random times before games. On this game-day, Bouncer Guy, who works until six in the morning is oversleeping-absent five minutes before the opening whistle. Same tardiness for the Dane who drives a bomb that broke down. I keep alternating my gaze between the club entrance, our twelve players, and the twenty-five Stallions licking their chops primed to exact their revenge on us—and more important to my skeletal structure, on me!

Their kicker is a good one. He's also their offensive and defensive end, and the same guy who was pawing my glasses earlier. He works for their version of the CIA, hence the nickname. He blasts the kick out of the end zone. We have the ball at our 20. With a lot of luck and effort, our first running play leaves us only one yard behind from where we started. The next play begins with me fading back to pass and ends with me prone, squinting into the sun after a 10-yard loss. On 3rd and 15, Greg moves to QB and gets sacked at our 1. We punt it short and the same CIA guy picks it up and runs it for a touchdown. He kicks the extra point, making it 7-0 them.

CIA squiggles the kickoff to our 4, where Homer juggles it and finally falls on it. On the next play, I hand it back to him, and he struggles ahead for 3. From shotgun, I roll to the right and for my life. I miss Greg at our 10 yard line. Greg rotates back in at QB. I heard he ran it twice, resulting in a 1st down. I missed it, as I was occupied staring at the club entrance. *Where in the F are you two?* I come back in and intentionally toss one high to Raul, as he is well defended by a shorter corner; he gets both hands on it but can't pull it in. Greg thankfully gives me a one-play respite from the onslaught, and he takes the sack of 5 yards. Back in, I roll left out of the shotgun; I finally feel I have a little time. As I scan the left side of the field, unbeknownst to me CIA is running full speed in my direction. He launches all his 6'3" and 225 pounds onto me, pile-driving me into the ground. I don't feel hurt, yet as I am slowly digging myself out of the hole I was buried in, I remember Jim Brown saying in an interview something to the effect of, "I always got up slow, so they wouldn't know when they really got me." I imitate; I guess I was too dizzy to factor the following: Prior to this one, I always tried to get up quickly after hits. Damn, I should have given him the glasses! The ref runs over to check on me like it was a standing eight in a boxing match. We have a bad snap on the punt and are lucky to get a 10-yard net gain on the punt after their return.

A QB run goes for 7. They follow with a short pass to their halfback in the end zone. They kick the extra point to make it 14-0 them.

We start at the 20. In shotgun, the ball is snapped over my head, and only a lucky bounce has me recovering it and running in the direction of the line of scrimmage. I break two tackles and fall forward to get back to it. Wherever I look, they are coming. Generalisimo Custer, I know how you felt, dude. I get sacked on the following pass attempt.

Another touchdown later, the half ends 20-0 them. We are too shell-shocked to get down as we realize how badly we are outmanned. The most enjoyable halftime show I have ever seen is The Dane and Bouncer guy marching in unison toward our beleaguered sideline.

Before the second half begins, CIA announces to our team, "Boy, my leg is tired." By this he means: From having to kick off after so many touchdowns and boot so many extra points, his leg is worn out.

They stall on their first drive and then boom a punt to our 15, where we down it. On 2nd down, I hand it to Homer, playing in his last game. He appears stuck in first gear as he struggles to break through their line; when he does, it's off to the races. With nobody else laying a hand on him, he sprints 80 yards for a touchdown. I pitch it out to Greg, who is stopped on the conversion attempt, whittling their lead down to 20-6.

Our defense shuts down their drive, and they have to kick it back to us. After the touchback, we soon have it at our 35. I pitch it to Homer, who goes around the left side for ten. Two returning linemen later and we are looking like our old selves. I'm thinking, *No wonder the NFL prizes them so highly.* Even our old selves stalled now and then, and that's what we do, forcing us to punt.

Arnold runs down and makes yet another special-teams tackle at their 14. Their QB when under pressure has a bad habit of running backward, rather than throwing it away or taking the hit to limit the loss. On 3rd down he validates my assessment by falling to the ground at the 1. They have to kick from their end zone. I could not have picked a better place for them to fumble it and fall on it for a safety. Since 20-8 is a little more respectable, they elect to punt it back to us.

After a few runs, on a quick count I get the ball in shotgun. I loft a high archer toward Raul in the right corner of the end zone. As the ball is in the air, Stewart screams, "That's yours Raul!" How right he is, it drops right into his hands for 6 points.

Believe it or not, unless verbally provoked, I'm normally not one for running my mouth after making a good play. As a matter of fact, I often feel self-conscious yelling the snap count because it's cliché trying to sound macho during that task. Nevertheless, I am castigating no one in particular as I blurt out my muffler-less thoughts: "Don't you dare put me in a hole, don't you dare, because this is what you are going to get!"

We miss the 2, so it's 20-14 them. Their next possession stalls and they punt, and without any of us near it, we watch it roll to our 20.

Three runs move us to the left hash mark at their 31. Out of the shotgun, I throw an instant replay of Raul's touchdown reception to Greg. As the ref raises his hands above his head to signal the touchdown, I notice a linebacker putting his hands on his hips in frustration from this repetition. I rarely take pleasure from an opponent's suffering. Yet seeing this makes me think, *You've got these guys backpedaling, time to move in for the kill.* Our Esteban misses that memo and the handoff, fumbling the 2-point conversion away. Rather than pick up the loose ball and try to run for 2 points with it, another one of our players with nobody else near him just falls on it. As the offense is coming back to the sideline, Homer's girlfriend spits the chewing gum out of her mouth in the process of screaming, "C'mon, you F'n dumb-asses!"

It seems like just yesterday I was spending Saturdays reading the *New York Times* at outdoor cafés on Columbus Avenue. Yeah, I know, I bitched worse about that crowd . . .

A 20-20 tie.

Apparently the Stallions did not get my backpedaling memo either and march down the field, culminating with their QB's multiple-tackle-breaking run around the left side for the score. Their sideline is hollering "BOO!-JHAA!" as if it were they who came back from the dead. The thought of having something so cool-sounding as the new cheer, BOO!-JHAA!, to add to my repertoire slightly softens the blow. Flippant I know, but I loved the sound of it. Hey, I can't control everything going on inside my helmet, less so after a year and a half of getting it slammed. It's 26-20 after they miss the extra point.

Homer runs the following kickoff back to our 30. Greg calls a reverse that deep in our territory. The exchange gets fumbled but bounces right back up to Greg. CIA, with his head pointed down searching the ground, loses sight of the ball and gains sight of a pair of legs. He grabs them and smashes his victim to the turf. He only stops his celebration when he realizes that it was their other defensive end, oops! I see another defender also confused and block him. I actually say, "Take that!" I cringe while thinking about my choice of words; I'm relieved as I realize he probably did not understand me. As I spot CIA walking back to his huddle, I shout, "Oh God, I pray they don't let you carry a gun!" I miss a few passes and our ensuing punt is partially blocked.

They take over at our 35, with around three minutes remaining. We have two time-outs left. The QB runs twice, netting seven yards. On the next play, we blitz him. He tries to avoid the ambush while holding the ball away from his body like a loaf of bread. Victor punishes him for that maneuver by slapping it out of his hand. They recover it at our 39, but they're facing 4th down. Their punt results in a touchback, and we begin the drive down 6 points at our 20 yard line. We now have one time-out left and less than two minutes remaining.

Greg runs for the sideline, picking up 5 yards. He doesn't get out of bounds and has to stop the clock with our final time-out. The next play is a *fly* pattern otherwise known as a *bomb* or *jet* to Raul. He has two steps on the defender. The pass is a few feet to the inside; by the time Raul looks up for it, he doesn't have time to adjust. Incomplete. I'm mad at myself for the big miss. On 3rd down, they are in a prevent defense with a three-man line. I take the snap in shotgun and scan the field looking for Greg, my intended target. He's double-covered; I look downfield for a split second more, then tuck it, and run toward the right sideline. I step out of bounds after a 13-yard pickup.

I set up the same on the next play. This time around, the call is for a sideline pattern to Raul lined up on the left, alongside Greg in our *twins* formation. Just before I start the snap count, I notice that in the process of making sure Greg or Raul won't burn them, they are leaving the right side of the field wide open. The second I get the ball, I turn and look left to sucker their right defensive end, CIA, into not doing his job of containing the outside run. He bites on the gambit and runs straight for me. I time his concussive presence, step forward, and he runs past me, Toro! With no further hesitation, I run for the right sideline again. I hear My-Boy for the first time wailing in English, with the same goofy voice I use when saying *That's my Boy*, "Look at Mike!" I feel special that he has learned the translation of "Mira Mike" just for me as I am getting wacked out of bounds. This edition of the same picks up 14. Considering how far back I started and the distance to the sideline, essentially I just ran two 40-yard sprints with a good smack to culminate the second. I jog back to the huddle and past it, telling Greg to take over.

As I'm fighting to regain my wind on the sideline, Greg misses a pass to Raul. The majority of times when he comes in at QB, he runs the ball himself out of shotgun. Their defense has now shifted to key on Greg at QB, who they rightfully fear is going to do what I just did but better—and burn them for 6. From their 35, Greg catches the snap and scrambles around, dodging tacklers for a good six seconds before spotting Raul in the end zone. He tosses it as far and high as he can, and Raul pulls it in for 6 points and a tie with less than a minute to go in the game.

I wanted back in on the conversion, but Greg comes in on most of those anyways. Greed is a good thing in football. I want to be around players that want the ball in tough spots. We miss the game-winning conversion: 26-26 tie. I was dying to fake a handoff to Greg up the middle, and bootleg right and drop a pass to tight end Sergio. I never second-guess Greg, who has been calling a perfect season. Hindsight is a radial keratectomy. Even without Phil Jackson on the sideline, I knew how to Zen the madness into slow motion. The last thirty seconds tick off, and we head to overtime.

In overtime, there is no kickoff; the ball is placed on the opponent's 30. We win the coin flip, and Greg at QB marches us down to the 5. From there, he rolls right and hits Sergio for a touchdown. We make the 2-point conversion, and it's now 34-26 us. They need a touchdown and the 2 points to tie.

On 3rd down and 10, their QB hits his star halfback on a short pass, and he runs it all the way in for 6 points. They line up for the potentially tying play. I had never played a down of defense this year, yet I wished I was in there, just so I would not have to suffer watching it from the sideline. Their halfback powers the conversion up the middle for a 34-34 tie.

In the second overtime, Greg hits Sergio again for another touchdown. We make the conversion and its 42-34 us.

On their first play, they throw another short pass to their halfback; he puts the ball right back in the end zone and keeps me in sideline hell. The score is 42-40 us. On the potentially game-tying 2-point conversion, we blitz. As the QB is rolling to his right and two tacklers are almost on him, rather than heave the ball into the end zone and hope for the best, he takes the ball to the ground with him and they lose. Throughout the season, he had thrown a ton of interceptions on balls he should have swallowed or tossed away intentionally, yet rather than heave the requisite Hail *Maria*, he fell harmlessly to the ground without trying to get the ball out of his hand.

Part of me wanted to ask the QB, *Do you think you might have done better than getting shutout last year by Paraguay if you had swallowed your pride instead of Gustavo's schlong and let me play QB and Greg receiver? Do you think you might have done better had you listened to my humble advice about your moronic playbook?* More of me felt sorry for him as

I congratulated him on the great game that he had until that last play. Other than the two games against us, he played poorly at QB all year; on defense he was a terror. I was also tempted to have a T-shirt made for CIA: *Boy my leg felt tired* printed on the front, and on the back, *and now my ass feels exhausted.* I could not think of a more productive way to spend my time and money, but I didn't want to offer up further motivation if we were to meet them in the play-offs. I was hoping we wouldn't have to.

After showering, I was still hopped-up from the victory, so I sat in my folding chair and watched the second game. Mistake. I was back in bed sick until Tuesday.

NATIONAL TEAM VS.
PARAGUAY

We finished the first part of the season with six wins and no losses. No more games the next four weeks. The league called this sabbatical for National team tryouts and practices, culminating with the game in Paraguay, whom Argentina has never beaten.

Greg decides to just have a short team practice the following Wednesday and go out for beers afterward. At our practice, Esteban and Sergio walk over and tell me that yesterday they went to the invitation-only tryouts for the National team. They are coached by Dario of my old team, the Gladiators. I am hurt at not being invited, but rationalize that if our offensive line is as porous as it has been in previous years, the running QB of the Toros is probably the better choice. I ask them which quarterbacks were invited to the tryouts. They list every starting quarterback in the league with the exception of me. They were told to tell ex-NCAA Division I receiver Greg that he is invited to try out as a linebacker. My guess:

Gustavo is buddies with the Toros' QB, who I assume wanted his team's receivers for the National team, and Gustavo obliged him.

I finished the first half of the season with a QB rating of 119, the closest competitor from another team rated a 73. I threw six touchdowns and one interception. The closest competitor had three touchdowns and three picks. I completed 58 percent of my passes; the guy with the next highest percentage was Greg, with 50 percent. From the opposing teams, nobody completed over 42 percent. All of the four quarterback sneaks I attempted went for 1st downs. My average gain on planned runs was 7.2 yards. I believed Coach Dario held no animosity toward me; I assumed Gustavo and likely Manuel, too, were behind this slight. Paraguay had a real stadium and fans. By leading my adopted country to its first victory there, I could have taken this fantasy to a whole other level. I had to remind myself that within this culture, Vince Lombardi's quote "Winning isn't everything; it's the only thing" is typically viewed more in an individual, rather than a team, context. The pain in my throwing shoulder had increased to the point that I couldn't have played even if paid to do so. But that didn't lessen the rage I felt from the smallness of the league's brain trust.

X-rays and the magnetic resonance showed a slap tear. As I found out from www.cartilege.org: "A slap tear is an injury to the labrum of the shoulder, which is the ring of cartilage that surrounds the socket of the shoulder joint. Your shoulder is a ball-and-socket joint made up of three bones: your upper arm bone (humerus), your shoulder blade (scalpula) and your collarbone (clavicle)." Surgery was the cure. My physical therapist is doubtful that he can strengthen it enough to last through the season.

A highly rated shoulder specialist sticks a needle filled with cortisone in the back of my shoulder. I am slightly put off by the unexpectedness of his route. I pray the stuff lands where it's supposed to. He warns, "This is a one-time shot, and the next time your mobility is this limited, you will need to repair it with surgery. You should know that by playing with the shoulder in this condition you risk adding more screws and borrowing ligaments from other parts of your body to put it back together." He had trained in the United States and once was part of a team that operated on Coach Bill Belichick's players. He continued, "It would be highly unlikely that an NFL team would risk playing a quarterback with this injury, as further damage could permanently weaken the arm."

I considered the following: Neither Belichick nor any NFL scout had found their way to watch my fifty-two-year-old self play along with the other stumblebums. All the energy I had put into starting this team and helping it to the six wins without a loss. The level of confidence and the strength of the bond the Vikingos were gaining with each win. With Homer leaving, they would be counting on my arm even more. Most important, by describing my decision to play at all costs as a no-brainer, I would get to prove that, in fact, I had no brains.

Taking a twenty minute taxi ride to the place where I paid money to repetitively pull oversized rubber bands while counting to ten for an hour a day, four times a week, is not my ideal way to spend time. Boredom has me chatting with whomever comes close. I avoid the old games with the rugby players, because my arm would now be far easier for them to pull off and put on their lunch table. The gains come slowly, but this four-week break is a godsend.

At our next team practice the following week, Esteban informs me that the Toros' quarterback and Dario are butting heads. The National team is regressing. No patriotic spirit here, his words fill me with joy. I obsess about contacting the Paraguayan team to tell them a concocted story about being in the process of moving to Paraguay, show them game film, and try out for their team. I most certainly would have, had my shoulder been up to it. An Argentine loss against Paraguay would put them in a 3-0 hole against them. I pray for it, and fantasize even harder that I could be a part of making that happen.

During the second week of our four-week sabbatical, I get a call from Gustavo. "Would you be willing to help with the National team as Dario is having trouble getting players to see things his way?"

I answer his question this way: "Why wasn't I invited to try out for the team?"

As comes as no surprise, he defers, "That was a coach's decision."

I soften a little before I have time to understand that it's likely a lie. Unprompted, he throws more *I'm innocent* bullshit at me. Still my moral compass points me to responding, "I don't care how it went down, I am going there to help my friends."

I ask him what the problem is. He responds, "Dario and Guillermo, the Toros QB, are not seeing eye to eye."

Almost instantly, I figure out the reason. Depending on the pass play, Dario is set on a three, five, or seven step QB drop back. Guillermo is the Wildman of Borneo of quarterbacks; he is used to moving to where his instincts take him. Dario's path to success comes by being regimented. I show up to the next National team practice and sit in Dario's car with him to talk things over. First off, I ask him why I wasn't invited to the tryouts.

"I told Gustavo that I wanted you on the team."

Dario has no guile; I know he is telling the truth. I drop the matter then and there, because even if he were to lobby the league on my behalf, I can't play with my secretly damaged shoulder. With the exception of Greg and Raul, not even my own teammates know the extent of my injury. My allegiance is now to my old Coach Dario, whom I like and respect. With the rift between the coach and Guillermo, the Toros' QB, and disregarding my hidden shoulder injury, clearly I would have been his selection for starting quarterback for the National team.

At the practice, everything I believed is being proven in front of my eyes. Dario is having me teach him the various drop backs, and Guillermo looks more ready to drop out than back. As for their differences in philosophies, I don't say much. I just observe. After practice I speak with Greg on the phone and tell him the problem.

His simple solution goes like this: "They're going to win or lose the game on Guillermo's legs, let him do what he wants, turn him loose."

In desperation, Dario and Santiago come over to my house to talk it over. After pouring them a coffee, I tell Dario straight out, "You're trying to jam a square peg into a round hole. You're going to win or lose the game on Guillermo's legs, turn him loose."

It was as if he needed that borrowed cold slap to the face. I could see him admitting to himself that I (well, Greg, really) nailed it. "Your words are kind of tough, but I have to admit you are right."

The coach put his pride and standard methodology aside and accepted the solution. That's all it took to pull me completely on the team's side and to try to get Guillermo's head back in the game. Practices breezed along. I encouraged Guillermo, "Unless the game situation screams not to, tuck it and run whenever you see an opening."

There were five titled coaches on the team, so I was called "assistant to the offensive coach." Manuel was the offensive coach. The QB's best receiver was also a Toro. He was about 6' tall, and had played semiprofessional basketball and had the jumping ability that goes along with that. I couldn't resist showing the two of them a play Greg had taught me. In his words, "If the defender crowds me at the line of scrimmage, look for my hand opening and closing as a signal, then scratch the called play, and just loft it to me the second I get around him." They tried it a few times and weren't completing it. The defender blocking the receiver at the line was throwing off the QB's timing. I knew my jacked shoulder would not let me demonstrate it with my normal throwing motion. Instead I yelled hut with the ball in my hands, signaling the receiver to take off while facing in the completely opposite direction of him. I never turned around to face the play. While using both hands, I underhanded the ball back over my head as high and far as I could, like a backyard basketball trick shot. The receiver ran under it and caught it. The QB laughed and seemed to get it.

"Don't make it hard on yourself, put more air under it, lob it up there past the defender, and let it be the receiver's problem to run under it or out jump the defender for it. If you lob it quick and the defender keeps blocking him, you should get an automatic 1st down on the pass interference call." I felt a little like a traitor to my team, but this seemed a perfect play for their respective abilities.

Rather than rent a newer, more comfortable bus to Asunción, the league rented a jalopy that looked and rode more like a school bus; it added three hours to the now twenty-hour trip. They put that stress on the team to save money. Most of the players were pretty subdued and tried to sleep, Manuel was chewing my ear off about the offense; I looked out the window and tried to translate road signs in my head. To hell with that jittery, yap-happy, time waster; I knew Dario would be calling the plays so no need to bother with him.

We had a team dinner and then got together in the hotel conference room. All the coaches spoke to the team one by one. When my turn came, I encouraged them to keep the violence between the whistles and avoid stupid penalties. "Play with emotion but stay aware of what you need to do on every play. Communicate as much as you can. Yell to each other to make sure you are being heard, but no matter how stressed you feel, don't yell at each other to criticize. We are a team of equals, so act that way."

The president was my roommate. We chatted a little bit, and then he fell asleep around midnight. Good for him, bad for me; his snoring was threatening to vibrate a cardboard pastoral scene off the wall and onto my head. Not being privy to what constitutes a justifiable homicide in Paraguay, I instead began suffocating only myself with the pillow in a losing effort to muffle his noise. At 3:00 A.M. I gave up, got in a cab, and went to a casino. After an hour or so, I came back. I went up the elevator and could hear my roommate snoring when I was three doors away. I walked out of the two-star hotel and crossed the street to a three-star hotel in search of quiet and a legitimate mattress.

The following morning, leaving my new seven-dollar-a-night-more-expensive hotel, I was spotted by one of the players. He took it upon himself to spread the news of my better-than-thou action to the whole team. During breakfast, a few guys were calling me "three-star Mike." Another threw, "I thought we were supposed to be a team of equals" back at me. Before things got too out of hand, I stood up to address the team concerning this mushrooming scandal.

"Please guys let me explain myself." I could sense their satisfaction in seeing me backpedal. "The only reason I moved to a three-star hotel was because I couldn't find a five-star hotel. Do not get confused, you are a team of equals, we, as in me and all of youze are not a team of equals. Think of me as Jerry Jones the owner and yourselves as lowly players." I slowly and repetitively jabbed my finger at my chest and repeated at equal speed, "Owner, owner." I then panned my finger across the room and stated, "Mere players, meat on the hoof. Are we clear or do any of you want to get traded to Paraguay so the team can save the bus fare back on your sorry ass?" Amongst the laughter, I heard a few say, "You go Jerry!" I'm sure it comes as no surprise that most people on that team addressed me as Jerry from that point forward.

⊨＋⊩

This version of a football field appeared an easy ten yards wider than the regulation NFL pitch. That led me to speak with the defensive coaches to make sure they were of like mind to spread their ends and linebackers out farther. "If they get around the corner it's buh-bye."

Concerning the offense, I impart this to coach Dario, "Forget about long sideline patterns, he doesn't have the arm for them on this kooky field. Even if he did and gets picked out there, the corner could walk it in from 50 yards out, because the free safety will likely be in another zip code. Throw it down the field, worst case; it's the same as a punt. No trick or complicated plays on the first series; let them settle down first."

In the same vein, I talk with the corners. Don't go for the pick or even jump in front for a bat down unless you are dead sure. If you miss, you can't count on help, and its 6 points for them."

Throughout the first half, the teams appeared pretty evenly matched. With a few minutes to go in the half, we held a 17-14 lead and had the ball 4th and 2 on their 48. Dario and I have been consulting throughout. On offense, I am the only person he is turning to. At this moment I wished he wouldn't have, but he looks at me to ask what I think.

The fence-sitter in me surfaces: "The safe bet is to punt and take the lead into halftime, but we do have the momentum and could put them in a big hole with another touchdown. Uh, I dunno, your call on this one."

I would have kicked it away. Dario put his confidence in the offense and his balls on the 48 yard line and went for it. The Stallions star halfback ran it for 18 yards and then scored three plays later. With the addition of the 2-point conversion, we take an 11-point lead into halftime. I could have used Dario with me at the casino late last night.

He didn't go into the locker room at halftime. No need for it. I have never witnessed a more emotionally charged room before or since. Players were banging lockers, jamming fists in the air. Nobody was saying much, yet you could be illiterate at reading body language and still understand that something special was going on. I was hesitant to open my mouth, as I wasn't near that level of emotion and feared bringing them down. Yet when things just slightly calmed for a moment, I relayed, "With the positive energy that exists in this locker room, you could probably beat the New England Patriots. Just remember, no matter how well you play, the ball is not round and can bounce in funny ways. Whatever will happen, the intensity that has gripped all of you must stay with you the second half."

I believed I met a force field of emotions that my words did not penetrate. I was relieved by that, as I felt those words might have had a negative connotation. I walked out and went looking for Dario, who was riding his own emotional high chatting with Santiago.

My self-fulfilling prophecy came true in the second half. In spite of outplaying them, a couple of funny bounces and a bad call had Paraguay with the ball at our 37, driving for the winning touchdown. There were four minutes and a few seconds remaining, I huddled as much of the offense as I could get together. Putting it mildly, they were concerned.

"Hey guys, if they score they will be giving you the opportunity of your lives. You will get the ball back and have the chance to go on a heroic march. I promise you will remember that drive the rest of your lives. We all have three time-outs left. Without turnovers, their defense hasn't stopped you this half; they're dead tired. You will flat-out run them over. I want to see you guys be the heroes." I pounded a few shoulder pads to get them back in kill mode. Studying their faces after I finally shut my mouth, I hoped my low level of Spanish was the reason they didn't seem any more upbeat than before I started my apparent soliloquy.

Paraguay's offense moves it to our 15, in the process forcing us to use all of our time-outs. On 3rd down and 3, with fifty seconds to go their QB fades back to pass; their receiver has three steps on our cornerback. He tosses a perfect pass on a post pattern to his target in the end zone. As the receiver is bringing it in, my nemesis on the Stallions, coming from his free safety position, knocks it out of the guy's hands. With so much room near the sidelines, I couldn't understand why they threw it where the safety had a better chance to help. On 4th down we blitz and sack their QB. We take over on downs, kneel it on the final play, game over, we win.

After feeling the relief of the outcome, my resentment of all that went down before getting here resumes. Still, I couldn't stop myself from telling the helmet-scamming Stallion free safety, "You flat-out saved that game, dude."

I avoided the celebration in the middle of the field. Instead, I walked over to one of Paraguay's American players and started a conversation with him. Ten minutes later, on my way back to the bus, Gustavo walks out of his way to thank me for the help. One of my strengths as a quarterback is I'm not easy to tackle; a feather could have knocked me over. That went a long way in taking the edge off.

At the hotel, the team had a meeting and whoever wanted to say something could. My turn: "There were some plays that had to be made to win that game, and you guys made them. There was also a decision in particular that if it had not been made, doubtful we win that game. Near the end of the first half on 4th down, Dario put his faith in you guys to execute. You did and without those 8 points, well you do the math. If you didn't get that 1st down and they took possession and marched the other way for a score, we lose, and Dario takes the heat. He had the confidence in you guys and the huge balls to take that risk. Let's hear it for the coach." They complied loudly and he began to tear; everyone went over to show their affection. Knowing how hard Dario had worked for this outcome and how much it meant to him, I felt proud to be leading the cheer. I only wished I knew how to sing "For he's a jolly good fellow" in Spanish.

For the return trip, the league splurged on a bus and train combination, cutting the trip to fifteen hours. I thought it should have been the reverse, as we could have used the extra rest time before the game. Thank God they got that backward. I cursed myself for leaving my noise cancelling headphones at the apartment. A few of the linemen jammed five players into the tiny bathroom. I'm all for acting juvenile, but when the packing team looked at me for the sixth, I told them in a dead serious tone, "Forget it, I'm gonna be punching, kicking, and biting." As they moved on to softer targets, the shaving cream crew appeared and turned me into the Michelin Man.

In the train's bar car, with their backs to me, I overheard the president asking the running quarterback, "Did Mike help?"

He replied emphatically, "Oh yeah!" A little appreciation went along way. I rationalized that in a National team game, maybe it was fairer to have an Argentine quarterback.

They convinced the train company to play the tape of the game on the televisions. That kept the maniacs in their seats for a while. A few of the players asked me to get out of mine and chat up three English girls for them. Language barriers aside, I was honored that they thought highly enough of me on that field of play to select me to quarterback the mission. That night, the girls and three of the players had dinner at my house. For dessert, I happily let them convert my place into a cheap motel. Touchdown! From unpaid coach to unpaid pimp! I was moving up in the world.

AGUILAS II: BOMBS AWAY

We had a bye week, so I had another seven days to rehab my shoulder back into playing shape. By the end of that week, it felt reasonably close to normal. Our first game back was against the Aguilas, who we beat by only 2 points in the first meeting.

Right before the game as the president and I were standing at midfield, he asks, "How do you think your team will do without Homer?"

Without thought, I growl back angrily, "We'll score more because the ball is going to be in my hands more!"

I didn't even realize how ticked I still was about not being selected for the National team until those words jumped out of my mouth. As the game began, I was completely focused, with my pads barely covering up the figurative and literal chips on my shoulder beneath them. Greg was better at understanding and accepting the collective mentality of the league overseers and never took their slights as personally as I did. Although he was less vocal, he was none too pleased about being offered a linebacker spot when he was far and away the best receiver in the league.

Greg catches the kickoff and runs it back to midfield. On the first play from scrimmage, I rifle a 15-yard pass to Raul on a comeback route. It hits him in the numbers, which appear to be attached to his jersey by springs because the ball bounces off them to the turf. I'm so wired that for the first time I start toward him snarling. Sergio grabs my arm and tells me to take it easy. He's right, and I thank him for it. After a large exhale, I toss a short sideline pass to Greg that he drags out for 7 yards. A short pattern back to Raul goes for a first. Next play under center, I fake a hand-off to That's-My-Boy; I spin around and fire a straight-line fastball 30 yards and hit Greg's stickier numbers in stride for a touchdown. The shotgun snap goes over Greg's head, and we blow the conversion attempt, leaving it at 6-0 us.

They have replaced the short, scrambling QB for a tall guy with a better arm. He has less understanding of the game but isn't as prone to panic as their previous QB. On their first play from scrimmage, they run it about 20 yards and then fumble it back to us. I hand it off to That's- My-Boy for ten yards. Greg screams, "Atta boy, Miguel," whom you know as That's-My-Boy. I like the ring to Greg's interpretation of his name but figure, *Atta boy, That's-My-Boy* would be too tongue-twisting long to be practical in battlefield conditions. So I let, That's-My-or My-Boy serve as both his name and sufficient encouraging praise. Those on-field deductions serve to lighten my mood slightly. The next play is an exact replica of the TD pass play, except this time Greg loses it in the sun and doesn't pull it in. I hit our lightly used tight end, Julio, for a short pass; he spins off a tackler and takes it 12 yards. I get the ball in shotgun for a called pass play. I see a hole and without hesitation run through it for 8. Greg wants to reward Esteban for all his hard work on defense and calls two more running plays for him that net 15 yards and a touchdown. I toss the 2-point conversion to Greg for a 14-0 lead.

The Aguilas call their own 20 home for three plays. They punt it back to us and as the ball is bouncing and rolling forward, the Aguilas are crowding around it. That's-*Not*-My-Boy decides to join that crowd. Greg screams, "Get the hell away from it! Get the hell away from it!" That's *Not* My-Boy doesn't respond to the order, so Greg, out of fear and frustration, screams, "Get the hell away from it, you F'n idiot!" If you're not a football fan, in a situation as described above, the returning team's player, in this case That's-My-Boy, should not risk picking it up to run with it as there are so many defenders around him that they are likely to force him to fumble it in the process. Even if he overcomes the risk and grabs it, he's not going to go anywhere with it. If the haphazardly bouncing ball accidently touches him, it's a fumble and the punting team can pounce on it or pick it up and run with it. That being said, the idea in this situation is for the punt returner to stay the hell away from it. In this case, where That's-My-Boy was already in the near vicinity of the ball, he needs to heed Greg's words and get the hell away from it! To our team's collective relief, Greg walks over to the rookie That's-My-Boy to apologize, and then explain the reasoning above.

We march it down to their 10; I come out. Greg takes the snap in shotgun at the 11 and hits Stewart, who drops it in the end zone. I'm thinking, *Catch that freakin' thing!* Greg keeps it and runs it in for a touchdown. We fail on the conversion.

I warn everybody, "Don't forget, we had these guys buried in the same 20-0 hole last time, and we ended up barely holding onto our balls and the win." So much for my pep talk; they march and score to make it 20-6 us.

First play of the series from their 40. Feeling pressure, I take off running, only to be clothesline-tackled 10 yards later. I toss a bomb to Greg that falls incomplete. Next play, I lateral to Esteban, who fakes a sweep and then heaves a high arching pass to Greg in the end zone for Esteban's first TD pass. The ball gets snapped over Greg's head on the 2-point try, so it remains 26-6 us.

On the ensuing kickoff, Arnold makes yet another ankle-grab tackle deep in their zone. An end around takes them all the way downfield to our 14. It's looking like another "shootout at the *not OK by me* corral," as they march down the field and hit their star receiver for the TD. No such luck on the pass to him on the conversion, so it stays 26-12 us.

We march it down to their 5, where Greg calls another handoff to himself up the middle. He cuts to the right, juking two defenders before sprinting to the right corner of the end zone for the score. Raul gets the ball stripped out of his hands on the 2-point attempt pass, keeping it at 32-12 us.

On their next play from scrimmage, the only thing they can get rolling is the ball on the ground. We fall on it at the midfield. On 3rd down and 3, I sneak it past their line. I twist out of a linebacker's tackle and just miss doing the same with the corner. After the 10-yard pickup, it's 1st and 10 at their 33.

I hate getting dragged down by one tackler; I always feel I should have been able to pull or twist out of it. Getting blasted into outer space was okay, even fun. Like the sensation you get when going underwater while body surfing and the wave tumbles you however and wherever it wants. All you can do is relax and enjoy the trip. Same here, when I get popped good, I don't feel remorse for not staying upright.

My-Boy takes it for 5 up the gut we have been bludgeoning all day. Next play is a post pattern to Raul; he gets two steps and I hit him for the touchdown. Greg comes in for the conversion and misses the pass to Raul. It's now 38-12 our way.

It's late in the game, still they decide to punt from midfield. Victor punishes them for their timidity by blocking it and falling on it at their 37. I come in and reward them for their poor decision by missing a pitch to Esteban that their fastest corner picks up and runs for a touchdown. They miss the 2, bringing it to 38-18 us.

With the big lead, we give Arnold a try as a kick returner. He takes it all the way to their 30 as effortlessly as he chugs a beer. I hit Raul in the left corner of the end zone for another touchdown. About four full seconds after I released that ball, their linebacker blasts into my blind side at full speed. After getting up off the ground, there are no high fives for Raul; I can't lift my right arm past my waist. The 2 added by Greg widens our lead to 46-18.

On their kickoff return, Arnold obliterates their return man and dirtiest player into oblivion. That guy was responsible for the cheap shot above. That revenge hit is the icing on the victory cake for me. With a minute left, their ex-QB runs a punt all the way back to salvage a little pride, and the game ends 46-24.

The president walks over and tells me that our point tally is a league record. That only serves to bug me because of a bunch of missed conversion attempts and Greg's loss of a sure TD in the sun. Being it's a record, I wished we could have scored even more to put it further out of reach. I settle for our seventh consecutive win.

Hard to describe how obligated I felt to all my teammates. I had grown tight with them, even those whom I haven't always described in the most flattering of terms. Many people have at least one irritating trait. I'm sure my barbed humor didn't play so well for everybody five thousand miles off Broadway. They worked so hard and counted on me so much. For all our team's attributes, depth was not one of them. I was the only guy on the team who hadn't played both offense and defense regularly.

⊨ ⊨

I take my doctor at his word that he will only inject me that one time, so naturally I seek out another doctor. I choose not to bore the new doctor with my shoulder's sordid druggy history. What he doesn't know won't hurt him; me maybe, but not him. He tells me what I had already learned: "The effects of these injections only work for two or three weeks." After that time, medical science's liberating voyage into my bloodstream and my shoulder's range of motion will quickly return to being mostly mutually exclusive events. The new doctor's theory is to take the shot now to help me to get through the rehabilitation needed to be ready for the play-offs.

GLADIATORS II: WANNABE SPOILERS

I'm sitting this one out, as is Sergio with a hairline fracture in his wrist. Greg tells the team he's resting my old bones, but the team is catching on that I'm hurt. We're in the play-offs no matter the outcome of the remaining games. I had learned to control my emotions much better in this my second year. Standing on the sidelines out of uniform reverses any progress in that area. I'm determined to end the season undefeated and untied. As I can do little to help, I'm reduced to a nervous wreck. I have no way to release adrenaline other than screaming like the wack-job I can't stop proving myself to be. The Gladiators are not going to the play-offs. Busting our streak would go a long way toward restoring the pride that their losing season had taken from them.

They run back a short kick to midfield and with a well-balanced drive find themselves in our end zone. They blow the pitch on the 2-point conversion, so they kick it back to us, up 6-0.

We start at our 20. Esteban hits some short passes, and That's-My-Boy is doing the bulk of the work on the ground. At their 24, he hands it to Greg, who punctuates the drive with a touchdown. Greg completes the conversion pass to Julio, putting us up 8-6. The half ends that way.

We continue playing punting Ping-Pong, until Coach Dario decides to go for it on a 4th down at our 41. We ain't Paraguay and bat the pass down at the line of scrimmage.

Greg, Esteban, and That's-My-Boy share the load and bring it to 1st and goal from the 9. Esteban at QB pitches to Greg. The Gladiators have read this one all the way. As Greg is about to get gang-tackled, he looks up and spots Raul in the end zone and hits him for an ad-libbed score. On the 2-point conversion, Greg is back in at QB. He tries sneaking it in and gets stuffed.

When Greg gets back to the sideline, instead of complimenting him on his creative touchdown, Stewart reprimands him for running straight into the teeth of their defense on the conversion. It's face mask to face mask time for at least a full minute. I stay close, as I fear it might come to blows. Stewart is out of line, but I avoid telling him so, as I don't want him to feel ganged up on. We suited up just twelve players for this game; obviously we can't afford to lose one, especially from the offensive line. It's 14-6 us, and I'm not smiling.

They can't get their offense in gear the rest of the way, and we keep it on the ground as much as possible. We win the game 14-6. I'm not thinking about the victory. I'm worrying about what repercussions are coming from the Greg-Stewart fracas. Second-guessing the coach out loud during the game is one of the fastest ways to destruct a team from within. Greg and Stewart see the big picture and patch it up behind the scenes. I don't get mad, I tolerate.

Stewart calls me up that night and asks if I'm going to kick him off the team, mentioning something to the effect of his being down this road before. I play dumb as to why he thinks that and laugh him off. I push the conversation elsewhere. I feel relieved that it's not just my leadership that's the problem. Not hard to deduce this isn't the first team on which he had issues. I wish I'd said, *Hey, you have the right to express your opinions and criticisms to Greg but just not in the middle of the game in front of the other players.* Of course he knew this, but I believe my avoiding the issue with him made me appear weaker.

LOBOS II: THEY STILL CAN BITE

S ergio and I are again confined to the sidelines. It's a super-windy day, which further complicates our passing game. The Lobos might lack for talent at the skill positions, but their line is one of the two biggest and toughest in the league, they tax your bones for every yard you gain. I felt like I could play, as my shoulder was serviceable from the therapy and the lube job. As I hadn't been throwing at the practices, Greg wisely chose to sit me out. This game is by no means a lock.

We start at our 20 with Greg opening at QB. He mixes short passes with a variety of different runs to try to keep them from teeing off on our backs. That's-My-Boy is getting most of the calls, as Greg has placed himself and Esteban in as much of a preservation mode as he feels we can afford. With the wind in his face, Greg marches us the length of the field, finally scoring with a perfect pass on a short post pattern to Raul. Greg fakes a handoff and bootlegs the 2 in; 8-0 us.

A few possessions later, they have it at their own 26. From there, the little guy busts one all the way to our 2. A quarterback keeper finishes the job. The mini-might runs the 2 in to tie it at 8-8.

We start at our 20. Esteban misses Raul on a short pass. Then he lobs a deep pass over the middle to I don't know who, and they pick it off. If the score weren't tied, this would be a boring game to watch. I jump in place to burn nervous energy.

On their first play from their 31, they fumble the snap and fall on it for a 2-yard loss. We limit the little guy to just 1 yard on his next attempt. They throw one over the middle that Greg picks off and runs all the way back to their 6. Esteban hits Julio for the go-ahead touchdown. Greg is stuffed on the 2-yard attempt, making it 14-6 us.

We keep our next four series almost entirely on the ground. They have three more, with none of them resulting in a 1st down. This chapter ends with our ninth consecutive win.

TOROS II: A NEGOTIATED OUTCOME

The positions for the play-offs are set. The outcome of this game will have no effect on who will play who in the semifinals. As a result, the president of the league calls me on Monday and says that we don't have to play the meaningless game against the Toros. It's not like the league had to refund tickets, being that there were none.

I ask, "How will it show on the record? Will we be nine wins and zero losses?"

He answers, "Yes, but first you have to call the Toros, who need to agree to cancel the game."

I do so immediately, and they agree it would be counterproductive to play a pointless game. I call the president back to make sure that I haven't been double-crossed by the Toros. By this point, I believe there's no such thing as paranoia; it's only heightened awareness. He confirms the Toros had called him with their agreement. I assumed they would; still, I feel a surge of relief. Albeit unspoken, an undefeated, untied season has become more of a goal as the season progresses.

I tell Greg, who then cancels the first of the two practices for that week. Thursday I get another call from the president, who informs me that if we don't play, it will go down in the records as a tie. I tell him that he cannot go back on his word after we canceled one practice and had a light practice scheduled for that night. He says he will speak with the others in the league hierarchy. Friday he calls back and informs me that now it will go down in the records as a loss if we don't play. I give him a piece of my mind for being a party to robbing mine. I was hoping my decibel-rich argument would push him into revealing who was behind this decision that I saw as an attempt to play with my mind. He didn't squeal, but I had learned enough to make an educated guess.

With our limited personnel, it would be only be for vanity's sake to risk playing that game. I call the Toros back who agreed again not to show up. No big deal for them; they'd already lost three games. We chose not to play and to take the loss that wasn't. Well after the season, they changed it to not appearing as a loss or a tie in the records.

THE PLAY-OFFS: VIKINGOS VS. AGUILAS

I scan their sidelines and see the guy in the league whom I fear the most: their monster lineman Juan. He's dressed in street clothes as a result of a bum knee. I'm relieved yet feel bad for him, because he's such a soft-spoken and likeable guy off the field. The key words here are *off the field*.

We are without Sergio, still healing his cracked wrist. The Aguilas win the toss and elect to receive. The ex-QB picks it up at the goal line and sprints to his 10, where Esteban ends his little journey by executing a perfect strip of the ball. We recover it at their 15. First three plays net 4 yards. On 4th down, the called play is to Raul on an out pattern on the right side. I catch the ball in shotgun, and as I'm trying to time Raul's cut, I spot their right defensive end bee lining it straight for me. I turn to the left and arch my back, as if I were trying to miss his tag in a game of touch football. He misses and falls to the ground trying to cut back. My momentum forces me to jog to the left and look for a plan B; Greg notices my predicament and frees himself from his defender by running parallel to me. While on the move, I flick it to him for the score. On the 2-point conversion, I couldn't tell you if I stumbled over my own feet or the center's; my attention was elsewhere. Either way that conversion attempt is squandered. On their next possession, they go 3 and out, leaving it at 6-0 us.

We take possession on our own 30. After taking the snap, I run to my right to avoid a lineman who has broken through; he snags my ankle, and I crash hard 5 yards behind where I started. Greg calls a fly pattern to him. I get it under center, and by the time I set, I feel more pressure than I'm comfortable with, so I let go of it early in spite of him being double-covered. Somehow the wobbling duck got over both defenders and into his hands. The ball stays in them until he hands it to the ref in the end zone seconds after signaling our second touchdown. Under center I drop back two steps, jump up, and flick the conversion pass to Stewart, who grabs it above his head for his first score of the season, putting us up 14-0.

The Aguilas run it back to midfield. They hand it to the ex-QB, who takes it for 15. On 3rd down, they target their star receiver; he just gets the one foot in needed in the back of the end zone, after pulling in a perfect pass. No success when they go back to him on the conversion attempt, leaving it at 14-6 us.

Greg picks up the kickoff on one hop at the 5 and returns it to the 21. After a short run on 1st down, I pitch outside to Greg, who cuts it back up the middle, where he spins out of a tackle and nets a gain of 30 yards. Esteban gives me a breather for one play and runs for 7 yards. I go back in, roll to my right, and loft one to Julio in the back of the end zone. He looks up for it too late and misses a chance at a catchable ball.

I like to use Julio on short, easy routes, because defenses normally are preoccupied with Raul and Greg. After he catches it, he runs with a lot of heart. Deep balls his way are risky. I also know not to fire any fastballs at him. Those minor disclaimers aside, he would be of great value to the team even if only used as the fearless and instinctive linebacker he was.

Esteban goes back in at QB and runs it 4 yards. I completely understand and respect Greg's methodology in trying to keep my shoulder out of harm's way whenever possible. That being said, I feel as if I'm losing the rhythm of the game coming in and out as a relief pitcher. Let that serve as the best excuse I can come up with for jamming the ball into That's-My-Boy's hip on the next play, resulting in a turnover in their territory. They manage a few 1st downs before the half ends with us leading 14-6.

Greg runs the second half kickoff back to the 35 and stays in at QB. He almost always takes the snap in shotgun. On 3rd down, Greg hits Julio, and he takes it for 17. I go back in and audible again away from the called pass play to a run up the middle. Esteban doesn't make me look as smart as I'd hoped he would when he only picks up 3 yards. On the following play, I don't make myself appear any more intelligent by getting entangled in my center's feet, for a 1-yard loss. On 3rd and 8, I spot Raul open on his post corner route. I let go of the ball, pinpointing a spot in the end zone that I hope he'll get to at the same time as the ball. As I'm watching my handiwork sail away, a 230-pound lineman rolls full speed into the side of my knee. My knee buckles sideways; I feel no pain, as the cleat was not planted. Some 40 yards down the field, Raul pulls it in for another 6 points. To make sure the knee is still functional, I lift it up and shake it all about while singing to myself *and that's how you do the Hokey Pokey*. (I can't tell you if my silliness is environmentally or hereditarily induced; I only know I get that way at odd times.)

Wedding practice now over, on the 2-point conversion I pitch it to the right side to Greg; he in turn floats a pass in the direction of Raul. Their star picks it off in the end zone and quickly comes out to the 3, where he cuts so that he's running parallel to the goal line. He leaves our team in his wake as he runs toward the other sideline. The only thing preventing him from taking it all the way to add 2 points to their tally on our conversion attempt is me. I've been timing his run and moving parallel to him. He is passing me faster than I'd anticipated. In full stride, I reach out and grab his numbers with my left hand and then my right. We run along at almost full speed for a few more steps, which was okay by me, as I knew I wasn't letting go and he was not about to drag me 97 yards to steal our 2 points. Just in case, I pulled myself to the other side of him and planted my left leg and then dove over it, twisting him to the turf. If you include the spins on the ground, credit us with a triple axel. This New York judge gives us a 10; the striped judge standing over the play makes no call. As I am reveling in my loudest cheer of the year, their star starts pulling on his collar, as if to signal a horse collar infraction. From the other side of the field, Manuel tosses his flag. They will get 15 yards added to their return. We are up 20-6.

The ex-QB runs it back to the 35; after Manuel marches off my penalty, they have it at midfield. They go back to the ex-QB on a slant, and we can't drop him until our 37. The next pass is incomplete, followed by a QB keeper that puts it at our 30. Then they hit their star at the line of scrimmage; he breaks three tackles, including Greg's, for the score. They just miss the 2-point conversion pass, bringing them it 20-12, still our lead.

Greg receives the kick and runs it back to the 25. Esteban is in at QB and keeps it for 2 yards. Esteban hits Greg at the line of scrimmage, and he turns it into a 1st down. The music stops in this game of musical quarterbacks and I'm back in. I pitch to Greg for 5 yards. Then I hit Julio on an out route from his tight end position. His aggressive run after the catch adds 16 yards to our cause. I keep it and go for 10 yards and another 1st down. At their 25, I pitch it to Greg who moves us to the 15 yard line. I sense that they're getting tired. I roll right and sense I'm getting stupid as I cut back into traffic and lose a few yards as the third quarter ends.

I open the fourth quarter with a pitch to Greg that makes it 1st and goal from their 9. Greg moves to QB and hands to Esteban for a 2-yard pick up. Greg keeps the next one and plows through the middle for the score. On the 2-point conversion, an illegal-motion penalty sets us back 5 yards, and Greg misses the 2-point conversion pass from there. It's now 26-12 us.

Our kickoff results in a touchback. From their own 20, in short order they find their way to our 15. Raul picks off the next pass attempt at our 2 yard line, bringing their drive to an end. One bullet dodged!

A few short runs that don't add up to 10 yards and we have to punt. Victor can't handle the ball on the long snap, and they recover it in our end zone. On the 2-point attempt, they pitch left to the ex-QB, who passes to the star wide open in the end zone for the conversion. The score is 26-20 us. A forensic examination might show we got hit by the ricochet of that dodged bullet.

They boot yet another kickoff for a touch back. From there, Esteban hands to Greg for 3. Then he short-arms a pass incomplete to Greg at the line of scrimmage. I come in on 3rd down and pass to Raul for the 1st down. We move it mostly on the ground to midfield. Their defense tightens, and we're facing a 4th and 1 at their 41. Their star is a dangerous return man. Plus, the risk of blowing the long snap again or a blocked kick validates Greg's decision to go for it. Unfortunately for us, their great line play successfully trumps that validation as they stop Greg at the line of scrimmage. We turn it over on downs.

With time winding down, they hit a slant that goes for 29 to our 12.

On our sidelines, I notice a half-baseball-sized lump on the back of my throwing hand. I don't know how it happened and it doesn't really hurt or affect my ability to open and close it. Before I begin icing it, I walk over to the fifty or so players from the other teams who were watching the game from behind a chain-link fence. I interrupt their viewing at this critical moment in the game by putting my hands together near the fence with the big lump on top, as if ready to receive the snap under center and I ask loudly. "Who wants to play center for the Vikingos? Any volunteers?" It cracks them up and, more important, me, too! It also sends a message to whomever is going to meet me in the finals (if I get there): I don't get rattled. If not exactly calm, I'm feeling elated, as if I don't feel the weight of my body. I hope my wisecrack will help relax our offensive unit also if called upon to execute a do-or-die drive.

The refs call a timeout, signaling the two-minute warning. We stymie two runs run at the line of scrimmage. Greg calls a time-out so that if they score we will have enough time to march for the win. The next run nets them 4 yards. Greg calls another time-out. They now have it 3rd and 5 at our 8. Their big QB drags half our team into the end zone to tie the game at 26. On the 2-point conversion, they do an instant replay of the trick play pitch to the ex-QB who tosses it to the star. I quote Santiago from the Gladiators and scream, "Oh no, not again!" They take the lead 26-28.

We take possession at our 22 yard line with one minute and twenty-nine seconds remaining in the game—and our season, if we don't score. We have one time-out left.

On our first play from scrimmage, I hit Raul for a 20-yard pick up near our right sideline. The ref windmills his arm, signaling he did not get out of bounds; the clock is running. I then complete a sideline pattern for 8 yards to Greg, who does get out of bounds to stop the clock. Then I flub one to Raul, making it 3rd down and 2. They blitz me on 3rd down, and I barely get the pass off in the direction of Greg. Thankfully it wasn't picked or caught because he was double-covered and not near enough to the sideline to get out of bounds. It's 4th down; their sideline is going bonkers. I hit Greg on a sideline pattern right in front of their bench. The completion takes us to their 22, where Greg steps out of bounds to stop the clock and the noise coming from their sideline. From there I connect with Julio for 11 yards and another 1st down. We get a holding call, setting us back 10 yards to our 21. Next play, I overthrow an open Julio at the 2 that would have easily gone for a touchdown along their right sideline. Every now and then, I feel as if my arm is dancing to its own tune. On 2nd down, they blitz, and again I barely get it off in the direction of Greg, who is only a few yards past the line of scrimmage nowhere near the sideline. He intentionally bats it down as he is being swarmed by defenders. On 3rd down, I roll to my right like Joe Montana of "The Catch" fame; I see Julio getting past double coverage in the end zone just like Dwight Clark. I float a pass over the outstretched hands of the defenders, and Julio leaps up for the ball. Dwight Clark is 6'4"; Julio is 5'6". It just misses his outstretched hands. In pressure situations, Joe Montana would often say something offbeat in the huddle to relax his team. I choose not to make a crack about the height difference, as I doubt he even knows who Dwight Clark is.

Our predicament is 4th down and goal from their 21 with less than eighteen seconds remaining in the game. Our season rides on one play for the second time on this drive. I come back to the huddle and tell them the truth: "Hey guys, I could not feel more relaxed. Let's do this."

I don't know if I am as claimed, but I'm not scared either. Greg calls for a fly pattern to him in the end zone. I can't see Greg, only his defenders. I have to assume he is behind them, so I loft a spiral over them; it's not like I have other options. Greg reappears, jumping up and making a Willie Mays–style catch over his right shoulder. The Toros are screaming at the Toros referee (the skinny guy I should have drafted) to call an offensive-pass-interference penalty, even though there wasn't a hint of one. They vocalized then and there that they wanted no part of us in the finals. He raises his hands signaling the touchdown. The Toros had beaten the Stallions in the early game to advance to the finals. We miss the conversion leaving it at 32-28 us.

I can't get an answer on the time left; surely there is only time enough for the kickoff return. Their ex-QB runs it back to our 30 and fumbles it over to us. Now thankfully we don't have to worry about the clock running in slow motion. I kneel it once, game over, we win.

The president pulls me out of the locker room to do an interview with a cable sports show. The guy starts with, "We hear you are the Maradona of American football in Argentina?"

"Is that a question?"

"Yes."

"That's the craziest thing I have ever been asked, to compare myself to the legend Maradona! It's insulting. I don't want to be any part of that absurd comparison. Are you crazy, me and Maradona in the same breath? He's an icon, a legend! That's the most ridiculous thing I've ever been asked to do. That's nuts, please!"

He sheepishly apologizes.

"You ought to be sorry. When did Maradona ever throw four touchdown passes in a play-off game while only taking half the snaps? And you want to compare us, what's wrong with you?"

After enjoying the effects of being set up, he went back to his script.

"Do you feel you will have a big advantage against the Toros in the final because you manhandled them the last time you played them?"

As I was pointing across the field to some of the Aquilas still standing on their sideline, I said, "We mauled them also the last time we played them. Take an EKG on me now to see how much negative effect that game had on them today."

I win the offensive player of the week award. Fortunately we have an extra week off. I double up on my therapy sessions.

THE FINALS

In the week leading up to the finals I did not throw passes to receivers at practice; I just lightly tossed it around. I didn't want to risk further damage, because if anything, the shoulder was feeling weaker. As warned, the positive effects of the drugs were wearing off. I worried about a lot of things, but in spite of not practicing for a month, I didn't worry about my timing. When I had free moments throughout the week, I practiced by visualizing all our pass plays in my head. Learning that Sergio was going to play in spite of the cast on his wrist was a major confidence booster for all of us.

Early in the week, Stewart called me to tell me how stiff he was and that I had to find him a masseuse because he was too tight to play as he was. Later in the week he called me to tell me how nervous he was. I tried to reassure him with "I guarantee you after what we did to them last time, they are more nervous than us."

We learned that Manuel and Salvador were going to be two of the four referees. Common sense put Greg and I in fear. He suggested we boycott the game if they are not replaced. Although I was equally skeptical of their impartiality, I nixed his suggestion, knowing we would go nowhere but backward with that move. We gave each other a fatalistic shrug before moving on to the next subject.

At the club, Gustavo and one of the Toros walk over to me while I'm alone crossing an open practice field. Gustavo, in a whispering baby talk, asks if I want to do the coin toss now. His weird tone and the fact that the two of them searched me out when by myself seems odd. The coin toss is of huge significance because it was one of the hottest days of the year. One sideline was completely in the shade and the other was totally exposed.

On an equally hot day the following year, I witnessed with my own eyes and ears a referee not affiliated with any team handle the coin toss the following way: The team that was known for being defiant of Gustavo selected heads and it came up heads. The captain said, "We take the shady side and they can choose whether to kick or receive in whatever direction." The referee corrected him and said, "You won the coin toss, so you won the right to be the home team." He then pointed to the sunny side and said, "That's the home team's side." It was enforced.

I lost the coin toss, and as a result the Toro chose the shady sideline; we had to go to the sun-drenched side. This is how I figured Gustavo played it. If I had won the toss, he would have asked me whether I wanted to kick or receive, and at best, we both would have had our benches on the shady side. At worst, they would try to push the same home-team sideline nonsense on me, putting just us in the sun. If we were to share the same sideline, each team would not be allowed past their own 35 yard line to avoid conflict. After rain storms, the shady sideline was a mud bath, so when the shaded sideline was in that condition, they put both teams on the non-shaded, drier side to make the contest fairer. To simplify, it was likely a case of heads I win, tails you lose. I wish I had clarified what we were flipping for beforehand.

Anybody who would be coming to this game would obviously sit by the picnic tables behind the fence separating the shady sideline and the shaded picnic area behind it. I spotted a small bench on another practice field. I brought it over and placed it under a bush where at least two players might get some relief from the sun. Gustavo walks over and informs me, "You can't have that bench, it's for the fans."

"Gustavo, no fan is going to sit on it; it's 95 degrees outside."

"Sorry, that bench is for the fans."

"No fans are going to sit on that; they'll sit on the picnic tables in the shade."

We went back and forth for a few more cycles of the same until I exploded at the absurdity of his demand. After I finished screaming, he walked away laughing, proud of his completed mission. When I realized the real reason of this exchange was just to knock me off center, I smirked and thought all the better, as a little tension release was a good thing. The aftertaste led me to think about what might be coming next from him and his striped disciples.

As I stood on the sidelines trying to loosen my arm, I had the sensation that my shoulder had to bounce over five speed bumps before releasing the ball. It had never felt that bad at any point since the injection. I willed my confidence past this and was anxious to get on the field.

Our first drive with me as QB stalls, and their first drive stalls. On our second drive, I was on the bench. Greg and Esteban are running successfully. We have it at their 25. We get two 1st-down plays called back to due to penalties. During this time, the Dane was screaming to the referees that a Toros lineman was throwing dirt in his face, but that only results in a third penalty against us as he illegally takes his helmet off on the field to wipe his eyes. Next, two Toros slam Greg into a fence 10 yards out of bounds and no penalty is called; Greg begins to flip out, and one of the refs threatens to throw him out of the game.

On 4th and 10, I come in for the obvious pass play. Greg calls for a bomb to Raul lined up on the right side. As we are breaking out of the huddle, Raul moves close to me and whispers to throw it to his outside shoulder. This flies in the face of Greg's directive that we both had demonstratively agreed was the correct side at that preseason practice. All season long, we had not practiced it once the way he now wanted it. When telling me this, at first glance you would think his face has an encouraging look, and as if he was letting me on a secret. It has a slight odor of a bad salesman. The thin mask melts off as he glances back at me while jogging to his position. I see a warped pained face, which appears to be hiding something. I have seen that hybrid expression a few times in my life by people close to me secretly pitching me my own demise. The implications of his two faces don't sink in immediately. I had just come into the game and was a little gunned up. I figure he must have seen something, so I go with his request. He runs out of real estate after 15 yards. We were in their territory and it was 4th down, so I let go of as if it were a sideline timing pattern. The defender picks it uncontested. I walk off the field two parts ticked off and one part confused. Only after the play do I begin to begin to understand that expression and the oddity of his request. I'm left wondering if our team's tailbone pads should have extended further down. I fear he has made a pact with the devil. I erase that thought to concentrate on the game.

Our defense holds tight again and we get the ball back. I sit out the entire drive until called in for a 2nd and goal from their 20. I take a sack I only saw coming at the last second. After I get up, Stewart, in full panic mode, goes off on me. "You had enough time—why didn't you get rid of it?"

I'm aware it's my avoid-confrontation leadership style that is coming back to bite my ass. I should have lit him up from day one. The fact that we were shorthanded and couldn't afford to lose a lineman is no excuse. I needed to have initiated a dialogue.

On 3rd down and 14, I spot Greg in the end zone, where he has fallen. Running the ball doesn't come to my mind, as I've been guarding my shoulder like it is held together by shoestrings. I lose track of the downs and panic-toss it, trying to hit him where I hope he gets up. Picked off again, another opportunity squandered. This one infuriates me, because I can only blame myself.

On their next drive, they run out of downs and punt it back to us. Greg marches us down the field until he gets picked off at their 40. I spot the refs, Manuel and Salvador, exchanging giggles right after that turnover. Greg has been carrying the load on offense. He's hardly going in on defense as the heat is extreme; I stay nervous on every defensive play he sits out. Standing with Greg on the sideline, I watch them throw a slant to their speediest receiver over the middle and he takes it all the way for 6. They convert the 2. Their drawing of first blood makes it 8-0 them.

We get the ball back and with Greg at QB, we drive it deep into their territory before they pick him again. They go nowhere on their drive; we go nowhere on ours. We punt it back to them. They have it at their own 17. There is only time left for one more play in the first half. Raul is covering his receiver man to man. Being that time is running out, the smart move is to give him anything short and to protect against the bomb. Can't swear he heard me screaming that instruction, because he doesn't acknowledge me. They call a down, out and deep, Raul bites on the fake, they complete the deep ball, and it goes 83 yards for the score. Raul knows football; I assume he just lost concentration. They miss the 2, and its 14-0 them as the half comes to an end.

On the sideline, we are all over heated. I can feel the Gatorade sloshing around in my stomach in a losing effort to keep hydrated. Stewart paces back and forth, fighting back tears while reciting some hokey inspirational poetry. I feel sorry for his wife, who seems upset seeing her husband under emotional duress. He recovers his macho and begins to pound his chest and scream at all of us. "I need the ball, I need the ball." The Keyshawn Johnson wannabe might have gotten it, too, if he knew how to catch and wasn't the slowest person on the entire field. I'm irritated to the extreme; I find his center-stage panic attack a major obstacle to getting us back on track. I avoid going over to calm him. I fear if he goes off on me during the attempt it might negatively affect our team's mojo even worse. I don't believe the opposition had a penalty called against them in the half. I'm guessing we were flagged around nine times.

During the second half, I get my second wind. I no longer let my shoulder be a distraction, and Greg is leaving me in the game. I'm in full attack mode. I feel unstoppable, like I'm being spurred on by a bagpipe band blasting away in my helmet. I'm picking up bad snaps off the ground and tossing them to receivers. I'm doing what I have to do to keep drives alive. Many are being ended by Raul dropping a 3rd down pass.

With about three and a half minutes to go in the lost game, we have it 4th and 12 at midfield. I see Raul double- if not triple-covered at the 10. I know I have to throw it. An interception deep in their territory is as good as a punt. I heave it blindly. It gets picked and they bring it back to midfield. I am cooked; I'm angry and completely frustrated. I kick at the ball in the downed corner-back's hands. I get flagged for the 15 yards on an unsportsmanlike penalty. The Toros march it down and score. They miss the 2-point conversion, keeping it at 20-0 them.

We get the ball back and start our drive on our 30. I am determined not to get shut out. I hit Raul on a deep ball in perfect stride 40 yards down the field, and he drops it. When he comes back to the huddle, he apologizes this way: "Sorry, I didn't mean to screw up your statistics." I have never brought up my stats to a teammate during the season other than at the practice at which I learned I wasn't invited to the National team tryouts.

Greg calls a run for me; it goes for 10 yards. He calls my number again, and I bust loose up the left side and then cut it back to the middle and take it all the way down to the 6 yard line before being tackled by the twenty-two-year-old American kid. I call a comeback to Sergio, and he brings it in for the touchdown. As I am coming to the line for the conversion, their American kid says, "Sorry about the refereeing."

I respond with, "You guys played great; you deserve the win."

Why try to chip away at his enjoyment of their victory that he certainly had no hand in other than playing well.

We were a good team that knew how to win. We were not a dominant team that blew everybody out. We could have easily lost this game on our own. We had the added pressure of being the undefeated favorite. Homer was gone. We missed him at linebacker and especially at halfback, as we needed another runner so that Greg could have played more on defense. They had another speedy corner who didn't play in our first game with them. I still don't understand the behind-the-scenes maneuvering in a sporting event that had no apparent financial consequences.

I commiserated with a few of the players and then started walking back to the locker room by myself. I notice Stewart speaking with a friend of his whom I knew and another guy I didn't. Stewart's friend and the other dude motion me to stop and walk over to me. The guy I know says with a grin, "Tough loss. Huh?"

Before I can answer, he introduces me to his friend, a tall Mexican guy in his late forties. First words out of his smiling mouth: "I can see you need some help at quarterback; I'd like to come out next year and play."

My urge is to pile-drive him into the ground. *Sorry, dude, just was curious if you could take a hit.* Or go into rant mode drilling him with, *We don't need another malicious and sneaky prick like your friend in our locker room.* Instead I respond politely, "They now have an age limit of forty-five. I was only allowed to play because I was grandfathered in and paid to get a team started." I thank him and continue walking toward the locker room. I guess sending them over for that reason was Stewart's way of thanking me for the effort I put into organizing, footing the bill for most everything, and playing hurt.

While Greg is in the shower and out of earshot, Raul is explaining to everybody what Greg did wrong and that those were the reasons we lost. Julio, Sergio, and the Dane are in agreement. I was overcome by a numbing shock learning that human beings could be so disloyal and ungrateful to the guy who taught them everything. It took an effort just to turn my head to look at them.

I retort with, "We would not have even gone 5 and 5 without him."

I GOT NATIONALIZED!

I was friendly with the top receiver from the Toros, who came over to watch the NFL games on DIRECTV the next day. I was glad for the company, as few of the Vikingos showed up for games. Greg must have told him or one of his teammates about my shoulder, because he asked if it had hampered my game.

I went with, "I can't talk about injuries affecting anyone's play, because if I did, I could tell you that we would probably not have made it to the finals."

"What do you mean?"

"You know Juan from the Aguilas, their monster lineman who sat out the semifinals with a bum knee?" He nods yes. I continue, "On that final drive for our win, if I have him in my face, good chance we don't win that game." I gave him a bottle of champagne to drink with his teammates.

⥌ ⥏

Four days later, I couldn't move my right arm and inch from where it hung. Five days after that, I had a three-hour surgery to repair the level four slap tear in my shoulder. They borrowed ligaments from my biceps to reconstruct it. At least that's what the surgeon told me; I was asleep. He informed me afterward as a separate issue that he was close to putting a plastic sleeve in my shoulder as my cartilage was filled with holes. It was a seven-month, four-times-per-week rehabilitation. A few years down the road, I had a "hip resurfacing," which is a new type of mechanical hip procedure in which they cut less bone. I will need another one for the other side in the coming years.

I was anxious to see the DVD of the game to further understand how and why our wheels came off. I also wanted confirmation of my suspicions of Manuel's and Salvador's selective whistles. The league informed us that the computer ate the recording and there was no DVD. To that date it was the only lost recording of a league game.

After Greg learned about that, he told me he was not coming back next year. That hurt. Neither was Stewart. That didn't. One of the new goals I set for myself was to put friendships ahead of everything, including winning. Another was to put the Latin Americans in the glamour positions.

That's-My-Boy had a barbecue at his parent's house two weeks after my operation. Getting in a cab for a thirty-minute ride in Buenos Aires' free-for-all traffic so soon after surgery was not appealing, so I bagged out. Sergio was pretty cool to tell me that some of the players thought that I was mad at them because I hadn't seen anybody since the finals. I told him I was just not feeling up to it, without making specific mention of not being angry with any of our players. I didn't think to give him a message to relay how much

I dug everybody. I was too busy moping about my pain, and the loss, to think of my teammates. I clenched my teeth and said nothing positive as I thought of Raul's expression moments before the right-shoulder bomb in the finals.

After unloading my thoughts on poor Sergio, excluding Raul's selective dyslexia on what had gone down, he countered reassuringly with, "But that's part of all sports." I'd lived here long enough to not be shocked by his tolerance of being jobbed.

During the off-season I encouraged everybody on the team to recruit so that we wouldn't have to deal with player shortages like we had this season. Word got back to me that Julio, the Dane, and a few others were encouraging others not to do so, as it could cut into the present squad's playing time. I didn't take up the issue with them. I just kept reminding all the players, "If you are interested in winning, we need bodies."

On the first day of the following season's camp, I was sitting with Julio and Jorge, the "owner" of the Aguilas, at the club's restaurant after watching the new recruits. Jorge was prompting Julio into joining him in busting my chops about being a dinosaur. Julio took the bait and a few lighthearted swipes. Jorge then asks me, "Would you trade Julio for a third-round pick?"

"A fourth-rounder if you pick up lunch, too."

Julio was clearly offended. I considered reassuring him that I was just breaking his balls back, but I thought, *Granted, my shot was a little harder, but hey, you got suckered into making fun of me and now that it comes back at you, you're going cry about it?*

Knowing how emotional Julio was, I should have walked over and put my arm around him and told him and the subterfuging prick Jorge the truth: *If Julio's not on my team, I don't want to be part of the team.*

⊨┼ ┼⊨

Raul was calling me every few days about starting practices three months before the season. I repeatedly told him that we would start formal practices six weeks before the first preseason game.

"It's a long season, and I don't want to burn us out. If any of the players want to get together informally, I think that would be great."

I believed I had to be firm with him; Gustavo had made him a confidant. He could now be seen following Gustavo as if he were his puppy. Raul's increased confidence, if not cockiness, was unmistakable, commiserate with his standing in the league's inner circle.

I stopped going to the rookie camp, because they instituted new rules. One: We could not talk to the players even during breaks. Two: We had to stand so far away we could barely see the action. Three: Only the Vikingos recruits could not have their names on their T-shirts. I never received a clear explanation on number three, but I formed a very clear picture. I stopped going and let Raul handle that part by himself. Two of the rugby studs I had recruited quit after a few weeks. Raul never mentioned this to me.

"Raul, why in God's name, didn't you tell me about this? At least I could have had a chance to talk them out of it. I spent money on the ads to get them."

He gave me no answer and would not acknowledge that he did anything wrong.

A few weeks later we had a team meeting at my house. Twice when I was speaking Raul scolded me not to interrupt him when

125

I hadn't. His open defiance had begun. I wasn't particularly worried because I figured the team would have to be completely blind if they couldn't see the advantages of me running things verses him. I didn't want to make a scene in front of the other players. My shoulder still being in such a precarious state also limited my aggression. I was more emotionally stung than anything. This wasn't a for-profit enterprise; this was about a bunch of friends trying to have fun playing football and do our best to win at it. I was recognized league-wise as one of if not the best facilitator of this. He fought not to smile after each of his reprimands.

Raul and I had worked together on finding a tailor to make polo shirts for all the players, embroidered with our logo and denoting our ten straight wins. I show up to our initial practice after it had started to surprise the team with the shirts. I call the players over, and Raul tells me to let them finish this part of practice first. I ignore him and call out to Esteban, and he signals me to leave him alone as he is occupied. Bingo, Raul's new coconspirator.

This new discovery especially ticks me off because at my playing time's expense last season I had pushed to get this guy more time at QB, as I saw him as the future. Esteban was well aware I was his top advocate. He had good fundamentals on defense and carrying the ball, but at quarterback he lacked. He would roll out for the pass with his head down, losing track of his receivers; by the time he looked up, the play as designed was over. When I corrected him, I made sure to do it away from the other players. I wanted him to be seen as an on-field leader. Before practice one day, he comes to me with a play he designed in which all three receivers run the same S pattern and end up in the same place. I discreetly explain to him why it is a poor play. Next practice he brings another pass play to me in which all three receivers end up together again. I'm dumbfounded by his not understanding my last explanation. Again, I describe how this brings at least six people into a small space, making it pot luck who winds up with the ball. He seemed frustrated by the second polite rejection.

Whatever new play I bring to practice, Esteban knocks it in front of everybody, with Raul backing him up. On one occasion I retort with, "Well the play as it is seemed to work fine for Bear Bryant." I could have been speaking about Yogi Bear for all the player's blank faces proved. Raul has been telling the team behind my back that I won't be able to handle coaching without Greg's help. Even before being warned about this by Victor and a few others, I deduced it. Various other players had approached me, nervously asking if I would be able to get Greg to help me. I spot Julio telling secrets to another player in front of me while looking at me. Clearly Julio has been bitten and now is a Raul Zombie.

The big Dane and then Sergio follow in step, blowing me off at practice. The Dane was a simpleton who followed Raul's every dictate. It was hard to recognize the Dane's betrayal, because he often acted stupid without help. There where plays last season for which we would get delay-of-game penalties because, in spite of everybody screaming at him, he would walk back to the huddle slowly or skip it altogether, lost in his own brooding world. Sergio was the surprise of the bunch, but I should have seen that one coming, too, when he giggly bragged to me about Gustavo letting him do some menial task for the league.

If you had told me a few years earlier, while I was walking my dogs in Central Park and going home to my modest apartment, that I would be living in an expansive French style apartment, soon be frustrated by a brooding Danish offensive lineman to whom I'd be barking snap counts to in Buenos Aires while sporting a bright red helmet and jersey, all the while fighting a native uprising, I would have said your imagination was drug-fueled. That's how life goes, at least mine. The way things were moving, I envisioned coming back to New York half-dead to tell my story to Rudyard Kipling's ghost for his next book: *The Man Who Would Be Quarterback*.

Anyway, the gang had formed; it was the young capo Raul leading the Dane, Julio, Dr. Sergio, and the Chilean revolutionary. Although the Chilean Poncho Villa wannabe was too headstrong to march in step with the four, he took their moves as a chance to come at me from another flank. I thought it a safe assumption that they were secretly backed and advised by one of the heads of all the teams Gustavo. With the exception of one or two fence-sitters, the rest of the team was behind me. Thanks to Manuel, the Gladiators' owner, switching allegiances to Gustavo, his "friend," the president of the league, was now a powerless figurehead. I knew that in spite of having a numerical advantage, I held the losing hand. Whatever conversations I had with Gustavo in hopes of being able to restore order to my team had been stymied by his explanation of some rule that worked against me. The year was not enjoyable. The Fantastic Four, as some of the other players had labeled them, often did the opposite of what I ordered on the field during games. They could care less about losing as a result. Partly by luck, every call of mine that Esteban questioned explained itself as they all went my way. He never once acknowledged my superior judgments.

That second year, after completing physical therapy, I played one complete game for an absent Esteban, a few snaps in another, and a quarter in two more. I finished the season leading the league again in every positive QB statistical category, obviously with the exception of yardage and touchdowns. We went 6 and 4, and lost to the Toros in the first round of the play-offs. They picked off Esteban three times. He moved back to Chile after that game. I had taken him at his word at the beginning of the season about his staying here three more years. Now to prevent him from coming back, I wanted to build a wall on Argentina's western border before Trump ever mentioned his idea. I planned on knocking a hole in it just big enough for him to push through the new medium-sized helmet he used that year if he ever found it.

I tried to set up meetings with all the mutineers individually. The plan was to start each meeting with what I thought I might have done wrong and question them further on the same before going into my problems with them. They only agreed to meet as a group. I should have known by this that they were committed to a hostile takeover. Why not? They might not have held all the cards, but they had the dealer on their side. The meeting began and ended, for all intents and purposes, with them telling me, "The whole team hates you." I couldn't figure out if they were that heartless or they were simple enough to swallow more of Raul's endless fiction.

After our championship game loss, I was highly motivated to start a new and professional league here. I contacted a law firm experienced in professional sports to help me set up the framework. I was in cahoots with the league president, as I wanted him to be the president of the new one also. We had various productive meetings with the attorneys. I would handle marketing and promotions, and insert myself wherever I thought I could help. All the teams' players would be independent contractors and share a piece of the pie instead of paying into it. My phone friend at Football USA was anxious to help.

I was in the middle of pricing out television time to get the league noticed in a hurry when the Fantastic Four began their antics. Their behavior was a reality check. If my own teammates could turn on me and the team for a whiff of empty power, did I really want to throw money at building an organization in which I would need the support and loyalty of multiple times the amount of people? Not my money, for sure. That's what small did to them, and that's what small consistently does to their country.

Before taking on the responsibility of running the team, another more experienced expat had warned me not to get involved. "The idea of winning as a team and yielding to the more qualified person will usually be subjugated to gaining control regardless of who is more competent. Their country, so rich in resources, completely collapses every decade or so for the same reasons. They have a shorter memory for favors done than we do, so don't set yourself up for a fall with expectations based on a culture foreign to them." The beautiful and superior aspect of these people, and one of the traits that attracts me to them, is that they are the first to admit their shortcomings as a people. They have the rare ability to laugh at themselves.

My third year with the Vikingos, I suffered through more insults and childish games. Victor, my gutsy jack-of-all-trades and one of my most loyal players, left for another team when he tired of the abuse thrown his way. I stayed because I didn't want to walk away from a fight and because most on the team didn't want that crew in control. Every thought and move that I made was predicated on what was best for the team.

Sergio was now the quarterback. As great as he was at tight end and linebacker was as bad as he was at QB. He would not accept help. I remember one play during which he was running backward before getting sacked while simultaneously screaming at his line for letting it happen!

I had learned a year earlier, our second with the Vikingos, that he had emotional issues. At a practice, I had asked him if he wanted to be the second-string quarterback and I would move to third string. He said he wasn't interested. I tried to encourage him to at least give it a shot. Finally he grunted his approval, and I worked with him for only the ten minutes he permitted. We were playing the Lobos in the following game who were terrible. We had a huge lead going into the second half. As Esteban was busy padding his statistics against a lifeless team, he fought me not to come out.

I had told Sergio earlier, "You take the first set of downs, and if there is time, I will take the next series after yours."

In case of an injury to Esteban, I was plenty nervous about the possibility of having to go into a play-off game without having taken a snap to that point all that year. I desperately wanted to feel the ball in a game situation, and all that I had heard from Sergio was that he wanted no part of it. I finally got Esteban to come out, and Sergio fumbled away his first snap. When we got the ball back, I went in. After a few more plays, the whistle blew and the game was over.

Sergio jumped in my face with tears in eyes, screaming at me, "Why did you humiliate me and pull me out."

I was shocked and felt terrible. "I'm so sorry, I thought you heard me that we would each take a series. I'm sorry I didn't think of it that way. I was just nervous about getting myself some practice and thought you heard me say one series each."

I looked over to Esteban to back me up as I had told him two times that I wanted to get at least one series each for me and Sergio. Esteban made no expression, said nothing, and walked away. I looked back to Sergio and said, "This season is about you guys. I don't have to play a down. I just thought you weren't really into trying the position. My mistake please forgive me. It was not my intention at all to insult you."

He would not accept my apologies, and he walked away crying. I went home that night and after giving it thought I realized he was not all of who I thought he was.

I still regret not inviting him for coffee before the third season to clear the air. Part of the reason I didn't: I was afraid it might have been embarrassing for him.

⊫ ⊨

I made a new girlfriend and found her more enjoyable than the likes of my teammates. Also I was starting to believe my presence was counterproductive, even for my friends on the team. I stopped coming to all but a handful of the practices. I hardly knew the five rookies. Midway through the season, they wanted to move Sergio back to his old position and try a rookie receiver at QB. He knew little of the position but was fast and had a good arm. I was surprised when Raul called me to ask if I could come to practice to help. The Toros where going to be the opponent this Saturday. Again my motivation was for my friends on the team, and the new kid was nothing if not nice. He listened and was an absolute natural. After the practice, Julio walks over to Sergio a few feet from me and looks at me smiling while whispering to him. I had been in the locker room with them, so I can assure you at least anatomically speaking they were men. It made me sick to my stomach; they had asked for my help and, after I gave it, rewarded me with sorority-house cattiness.

I went to the game and coached the kid the whole time he was on the sideline. The key was for him not to take off running hard after the snap but to roll out slowly and look downfield, to keep the defense honest, and then bolt. Fortunately he completed some passes early on. That also helped prevent the defenders from keying on just his running. We beat the Toros by two touchdowns, and the kid was the hero. I took a lot of satisfaction from that. The next week Sergio wanted the position back, so he and his cronies who had control put him back in there.

On a Sunday before the final game of our third season, That's-My-Boy invites me to a team barbecue at his house. I guess the

Fantastic Four approved this because I was now essentially de-clawed. Half my motivation for going was that my new girlfriend was lovely in every way. I wanted them to see how I was now spending my time. It was fun catching up with my buddies.

Later on a new player approached me and my girlfriend on the patio and said, "Only here could a team operate like this." The Alemania, as he was called, was an Argentine who had spent six years in Germany and played every season while there. The level of football there is far more advanced, and the Huns certainly don't lack for size. I shook my head and laughed in agreement with him. I was anxious to hear what he had to say. We made plans to meet for coffee during the week. He was worldly and insightful. With no added drama, he dropped a horror story on me that even my friends on the team had shielded me from. He described practice as a boot camp, with the four leaders routinely ganging up and getting in the players faces over minor mistakes. The off-the-field quasi democracy I had set up was history, and now no one but the four had a say. They led through intimidation. On the roster was a super-talented American running back with top-level high school experience. He, too, was not asked for his opinion.

Sergio, by a huge margin, had the worst statistics at quarter-back in the league. He had three times the amount of interceptions as the next worst QB. Between the picks and his chronic case of fumble-itis, he was averaging three and a half turnovers per game all on his own! Still he would not cede his position to the talented kid I had worked with. When the Alemania told me the whole team was ready to quit if things didn't change, I was saddened at first but then realized I had an opening to try to burn off the group that had hijacked the team. I told him I would take care of business at the next game. He told me to hold off and wait a bit longer. I couldn't see why. The curtain needed to be pulled on the four great and powerful Oz's. All the better if I could expose their deeds to the entire league. In the first year, we were admired for being the team without strife. I never made the other teams in the league aware of our problems in the subsequent seasons, so as not to show weakness. Desperate times, desperado measures.

In the first quarter, a fight breaks out on our sidelines between the Dane and one of the new players. When I try to calm the Dane down, Julio walks over to me and warns, "Shut up, you're not the coach." I didn't want to elevate the situation during the game, so I walked away.

Apparently the Alemania had told the new players of the experiences I, "the owner," had had with the four after our coffee meeting. It must have come as a revelation, as it gave them the strength to quit on the field. Not in the normal losing heart way; I mean they took the field to make a statement. The defensive players often would not make a move to tackle anyone. They barely went through the motions; they flat-out went on strike! They were clearly motivated by the fact that I was not in support of the Fantastic Four. They knew I was behind them. I was now experienced enough to understand that this didn't guarantee they would be behind me. I watched Raul visibly weaken at each successive symbol of their revolt. Panic was coming over him. He looked like he wanted to go run and hide. I went over and sat with Gustavo along the fence 20 yards away. We almost always got along well on the surface. As the game was ending, I thanked him for his energy in keeping the league going and then told him with a telling smile, "Excuse me, I have some team business to attend to."

After the game Raul called everyone over and started to give a speech to the players. I could see the tears form in his eyes as the players jeered and glared at him. He ate, slept, and drank football, and now his world was crumbling before him. His voice was cracking. The tears that had been forming in his eyes were now running jet patterns down his face. The scene reminded me of the brutal dictator Colonel Gaddafi begging for his life from an angry mob only to get a knife jammed up his ass. Raul in his pathetic desperation, turns to me to rescue him! He feebly asks if I wanted to address the team. It was as if he were inviting me to be the master of ceremonies at his own funeral!

Unable to hide my emotions, I railed ahead with something to the effect of, "You are a coward who consistently betrayed the welfare of almost your entire team. You have taken what was the best team and destroyed it for your own false gain. This team will never win or enjoy themselves if you have any control of it. You are lesser than any human being I have ever met."

It was not what I said, because I doubt many understood me; rather it was the emotion that rose from my gut and the way it screeched out of my tightened throat that had the effect. I did not need to enunciate anything; the players knew where I was coming from, for they were in the same place.

The Big Dane, Raul's lady-in-waiting, was the biggest abuser of the other players. He walks over to me, as nervous as could be, and tells me, "Calm down. We are a team. We're all friends."

I got up in his grill and started screaming as loud as I could, "No, you destroyed what was once a team. You are a coward and punk, and I'll break your F'n arm if you don't get the F out of my face."

He backed up a few steps and meekly muttered, "But we are all friends. We're a team."

I moved forward inches from his face again and screamed, "Just flinch, you F'n pig, and I will show you what a team me and you are."

About half way through that season, I had been worried that he might end up with health issues because of how fat he was getting. I had invited him to lunch to talk about eating healthy. For the main course, he ordered four scoops of ice cream. Clearly he was too simple to think up that stunt on his own. I took a highly educated guess that this menu choice had been selected beforehand by Raul to jack with me. Still, for a kid who had eaten around fifteen meals and drunk countless beers at my house over the years to do something so offensive when I was genuinely worried about him and trying to help him galled me to the core.

Next up, Sergio, in a soothing voice, asks me to chill out. I run over to him and scream, "F you and the gang you're part of. You're a weaker bitch than Fat Stuff."

His face recoiled; he literally turned and ran away. As furious as I was, I had to fight off a laugh at that wind sprint.

Finally, Julio mans up and walks over to challenge me and starts jawing in my face.

At a team meeting earlier in the year, Julio had lied to the whole team in front of me, backed by Raul. "Mike told me he wants to replace you guys with American players. He told me that you guys are a sorry bunch and it's only our fault not his that we lost the finals," and so on. He then stuck his face in front of mine in an obvious attempt to get me to throw a punch so that Gustavo could toss me from the league.

Again I am aware here on the field that if I throw the first punch I will be kicked out of the league and powerless to help the team afterward. I flinch, trying to goad him into making the first move. Gustavo who had to have been enjoying the fracas he in no small part was responsible for, steps between us when it seems like it's going to erupt. We keep jawing so long that Gustavo and the crowd walk away from us. I keep screaming, "Punk! Coward!" I can't tell you what he was saying as I was too busy with my own shtick.

Finally as he starts to walk away, the plan comes to me. Incite him with heavy artillery and when he charges, back away (if not run away) a few yards to prove to the hundred witnesses that in the end I tried to avoid his violence. Next in self-defense take him down and grind his face in the dirt to humiliate him. There is no one else within 30 yards. He's only a few feet from me when I say as calmly as I can muster, "Hey, Julio, you know your new baby girl?"

He looks back at me queerly; I continue, "Ask your sexy wifey who the baby's real daddy is." My mistake, for whatever reason that took the fight out of him; his face shrunk in pain, and then he shook his head in resignation. As he continued walking, I screamed, "You're more yellow than the rest of your gang."

Do I feel I went too low? Nah. You go to F and you get F'd. Bullies need to be beaten down.

Keep in mind, off the field I had once believed I was good friends with these four. On the field, we believed in one another, we counted on one another. Instead of giving loyalty to someone who cared about them and worked toward their success and happiness, they let themselves get led to Hell by the very two people who likely sold out a whole year of their hard work. They had been part of a tight team and the most successful program. They betrayed me for the opportunity to steal something I would have happily given them if they had acted with a modicum of decency and then simply asked. I would have loved to have less responsibility if none at all. This was not sport; this was an aberration of it. From my viewpoint the league became the toy of a guy who could control outcomes of games with deal making. I, as Greg did, would have gladly left after what I witnessed in the finals of our first year. I stayed because I wanted to help my friends where I felt my help was needed. As mentioned, paying to start a new league after experiencing the walking, talking, and conniving variables in my own backyard was not going to happen.

Surely there are other instances when I offended or slighted someone that I haven't described above. That being said, I had never yelled or harshly criticized anyone on our team until the Fantastic Four began openly defying me. My guess is the beginning of the end started when Gustavo got to Raul, or simply the meeting of those like minds. It was sealed when the young "revolutionary" in turn led two seemingly intelligent adults, a simpleton, and confused a few others to follow his path.

Immediately after my noisy dive into sideline psychosis, a few of the rookies flashed me big smiles. As I feared the Four's lies with a mania, I walked over to some players from the other teams. "If you want to know the story behind this, ask me or anyone else from our team. If you ask them, you will get fiction."

A few of the Stallions then asked me to coach them, as their QB/coach was headed back to Peru. That offer was akin to a successful surgery to my wounded heart. You will never meet a greater group of guys than they had.

The following Monday, the five new players came over to my house for a meeting. One rookie timidly spoke, "I know I am only a rookie."

I cut him off and said, "If you are part of the team, what you have to say counts as much as what anyone else on the team has to say."

He, as did all the others, showed immediate relief on hearing that. The guys then expressed their bottled-up anger and frustrations. I told them, "I will do whatever you want. I don't care if you put me back in control or elect one of you guys." In fact, I recommend the Alemania. He was not at this meeting. I wanted to leave the team in capable hands and was more than happy to put my energies elsewhere.

As I went to my water cooler, I now overheard the timid guy I had empowered fifteen minutes earlier whispering to the uplifted players, "Surely we are not going to be sold on this guy by a beer and pretzels."

I jumped on it. "I'm not selling you anything. I don't want control; I just want to help make happen what the majority of you guys want."

After that last snake in the grass, I was not even sure of that. As it turned out, he was one of Sergio's buddies. For weeks afterward, I regretted not grabbing him by the back of his collar and tossing him out of my door. Call it the straw that should have broke this hump's back.

At the meeting, I learned that Julio, the Dane, and "Coach Raul" now barely had a friend or supporter on the team. They were despised. Even with Gustavo behind them, they would have been easily been pushed off the Vikingo ship if not for Sergio. Sergio and the Alemania had been longtime buddies, and the Alemania was the clear leader of the masses. Sergio was the least hostile of the Fantastic Four and was still well respected by most. Thus I knew, and was mostly thankful for the fact: I was done. Raul and his mob were out of power, and that's all I needed to walk away smiling.

I had one small mission left, and that was to bust up the dismantled Vikingo Gang of Four and the Gustavo connection. I told a few friends my plan ahead of time, so it could be proven that I had no intention to enrich Gustavo. The planned conversation with him was a ruse on my part. I invited Gustavo to lunch and he accepted. With my cell phone on record, I offered a sum as a donation to the league subtly predicated on letting me remove four players from the team. I thought it would be an easy sell because I did not have to act; he knew how I felt about them. I wanted the four to listen to a recording of the guy they kissed up to selling them out. He was all ears for a while, but he didn't bite. The sting as I set it up was deeply flawed. In my overt enthusiasm to publicly disgrace him, I didn't account for the fact that Gustavo scraped change off tables for a living. The ridiculously high amount I offered probably appeared too good to be true. Especially to a person who lived in a spy versus spy world. I wouldn't be surprised if he recorded the conversation also and played it for them to prove what a loyal guy he was. And then again, maybe he was.

Raul became the whipping boy of the team. He also improved as a player and made the National team again as a defensive back. I take credit for both. He had a self-imposed rule. After dropping a pass, he would do fifteen push-ups. By throwing to him as much as I did, at the end of our first season he looked like Arnold

Schwarzenegger. I watched the National team's game against Paraguay in Buenos Aires. As Raul ran up to players to congratulate them after a good play, they would brush him off. I felt sorry for him and his pathetic attempts to be accepted again. My feeling toward him softened because his being rejected proved that I had made many friends in the league. He never accepted responsibility for his undoing. To the few who would listen to him, it was I who created his hell. If you don't know the type, you are probably under the age of seven.

The Fantastic Four were neutered. The Alemania was now heading up the team. He made the American kid the head coach. The Yankee called the shots in practice and at the games, no one else. He figured it out. He made himself the quarterback and ran it or handed it off 99 percent of the time. He might have thrown six passes all year. They won a championship that way. As I still had a few friends on the team, I rooted for them. In the years they have existed, the only winning seasons they have had were with Greg, then me, then the American kid coaching. At one point after the American kid went back home, I looked on their roster and they had only fourteen players with nine of them being listed as assistant coaches. If I had to do it over again, I would have titled all team members co-head coach.

Looking at the league and its players, coupled with my experiences here and the perspective that distance and a few years will provide, I often think that Gustavo is the perfect leader for the league here. YouTube the song that children were once required to sing in school here about the military dictator Juan Perón: "Perón, Perón, que grande sos!" (Perón, Perón, how big you are!)

Maybe it was for the best for me and my bank account that I learned who some of my teammates were sooner rather than later. But at the end of the southern hemisphere day, I have no choice but to take the responsibility for not averting the civil war. Before games when I didn't stretch with the team and was off chatting with Greg about strategy, possibly they took it as arrogance. I should have invited other players at different times to these mini meetings, especially Stewart. I believe I underestimated how badly I hurt his feelings by ousting him as coach before he even got started and then marginalized him throughout the season. My doing so might explain some of his behavior toward me. His blowing a gasket at halftime in the finals happens to pros also who are hell bent on winning. Maybe I judged him too quickly; it had been many years since he played. He might have gotten his football mind back a few practices later. It took me two years with one apprenticing under Greg to fully do so.

On the field, a football team can't function as a democracy. Thus, it would have helped if I had tried to compensate for that off the field more than I did. I shouldn't have moped so long after the finals and surgery. Instead I should have gotten together with the team more often to hear how they wanted to go about things the following year. By not doing that, I created confusion and opened the door for the problems.

As a coach, I should have explained on-field decisions they grumbled about after the game. I just expected the players to know that I had the best football mind on the team; I thought, *I can't be bothered with stupidity and insubordination.* But how were many of them to understand my calls, if they hardly understood football strategy? Compounding that oversight was that the vacuum created by my lack of explanations was filled by the fabrications of my tireless director of misinformation, Raul. Julio was the emotional heart of the team. I should have altered my course with him when I first realized that he might not be taking my caustic humor as humor. Perhaps even Gustavo and Raul, who both had plenty of attributes I admired, could have been won over. It's a stretch, but I wish I had made a bigger effort. Gustavo put in long hours helping to make the league tick. I know I didn't care for his methods, but I have no real proof of serious wrongdoings. I could go on and on with the introspection and the self-blame, but what fun is that compared to railing on others? The best thing to come out of the conflict was that it helped my first and recent marriage. Communicate or say bye-bye!

When you live in another culture and don't understand some of its differences, you have to go out of your way to learn about them—or go crazy. For instance, many Argentines seemingly, or at first glance, are trained during childhood to hold their neighbors in contempt and to disrespect their fellow man: One morning I was abruptly awoken at 5:00 A.M. with a thud in my heart almost as loud as the beating drum that caused it. I tried to go back to sleep only to be awoken by the same noise fifteen minutes later. On the third go round, I opened my balcony door and walked onto it in my boxer shorts ready to scream bloody murder. I saw, in rows of two, twenty-four ten-year old girls from the private school down the block. They were parading in their school uniforms, being led by the largest student pounding a huge marching band drum. As is their tradition, they were announcing the first day of school. I went inside and prepared my speech for their next attack. When they came, I screamed, "You are endangering the lives of your elderly neighbors, you're affecting adults' ability to function at work to earn the money to pay for their children's school. You need to question your teachers as to why they are teaching you to terrorize your neighbors. You need to question your parents as to why they are sending you to a school that teaches you to have no regard for your fellow man." They looked up at me and laughed. I checked to make sure I wasn't hanging out and headed to jail. It was just that they couldn't make out my Spanglish and that I was nothing more than a raving lunatic.

It later dawned on me that most of their parents had lived through the repression of the military government. That government had air-dropped more than thirty thousand citizens into the Rio Plata as a quasi mute button for the rest of the population.

Teachers were a prime target. Understandably, students are being taught to never be afraid to speak up and be heard. I assume most others on the block are comforted by their symbolic noise, knowing the coming generation is being trained to be fearless, as many of the prior generation were to stand tall against tyranny. By not understanding their history and culture, I was worse than wrong; I was loud wrong. I use that ad-hoc homegrown deduction to calm myself every time teenagers on the block are making a racket all night long. Police for that? Different culture again.

If you were to ask me—after the hip replacement with the other hip soon to follow, the destroyed shoulder and all the grief I encountered—would I do it again? With no hesitation: Hell, yes! My time on the field was the greatest thrill of my life. I never felt more alive and focused. Being a life-long fan well into middle age, to be able to lift myself off the couch and onto that field to experience the things that I did, makes me believe that all my dreams are still possible. More important, I learned so much, especially about the things I needed to do to improve myself. In the end, you try to learn from experiences and concentrate on going about it better the next time around. Please just give me three or four more lifetimes to rest up before that next round!

Canadian Postscript: After that third season, Homer and his girlfriend came to Buenos Aires for a visit. It was plain to see he had matured considerably. I learned in those few days and after a few lost chess matches that I had him figured wrong. There was never a lack of intelligence; he had just been suffering through a severe bout of teenage angst. He brought me a gift-wrapped sweatshirt from his old high school team and thanked me for my patience with him. Humbled, I laughed off his comments. My only regret now is that he doesn't live closer.

ABOUT THE AUTHOR

 Mitchell Belacone, a native New Yorker, has been living in Buenos Aires since 2003. A mediocre athlete growing up, he came into his own in his fifties as a league-leading quarterback in Argentina. When informed that John Grisham had written a book about an American playing in Italy entitled *Playing for Pizza*, Belacone responded, "Judging solely by a comparison of his book and mine; he should be writing for pizza." The preface will fill you in on many more details about Mr. Belacone. This mostly lighthearted football drama follows Belacone's well-received first book, *Two Dramas on My Way to Hell*, a collection of short stories based on earlier adventures and misadventures.

21557925R00093

Made in the USA
Columbia, SC
19 July 2018